HERITAGE OF '76

HERITAGE OF '76

EDITOR

Jay P. Dolan

EPILOG

Henry Steele Commager

UNIVERSITY OF NOTRE DAME PRESS

Jacket design and illustrations by Clif Peterson

Library of Congress Cataloging in Publication Data
Main entry under title:

Heritage of '76.

   "The essays initially appeared monthly in the
Elkhart truth beginning in March 1975 under the title:
'76 That's the spirit."
   1. United States—Biography. I. Dolan, Jay P.,
1936–   II. Elkhart truth.
CT214.H47   973'.0992 [B]   76–739
ISBN 0-268-01065-X

Manufactured in the United States of America

To the American People—Past and Present

ELKHART BICENTENNIAL COMMISSION 1976

Mrs. Chauncey Baldwin
Walter Beardsley
Rev. Lester Bill
David Bonfiglio
Robert Branscomb
Mary Briggs
Kenneth Cantzler
Henry Curry
Arthur Decio
Robert Dungy
Roger Etter
Fran Everett
Howard Hostetler
Walter Krumweide
James Kurtz
William Miller
Ella Marie Murphy
Robert Pickrell
Rosalie Raney Isenbarger
Frank Rizzo
Robert Schnuck
Glen Searer
John Stinespring
Edward Stuart
Joyce Vanderhegghen

Contents

Foreword

The commemoration of the Bicentennial of the American Revolution has been the occasion for numerous celebrations. Across the country local communities have observed the 200th birthday of the revolution in a variety of ways, making the Bicentennial the longest and largest birthday party that the United States has witnessed. The community of Elkhart, Indiana was not lacking in this spirit of celebration, but the chairman of this midwestern town's Bicentennial Commission, Arthur J. Decio, demanded more than parades, confetti and birthday speeches. Under the personal sponsorship of their chairman the Commission decided on a project that would explore the meaning of the spirit of 1776 by examining the lives of selected individuals who exemplified this spirit over the past 200 years and thereby provide a more lasting tribute to the observance of this nation's Bicentennial. The worthy nature of the undertaking found me quick to respond to the Commission's request for editorial direction.

With the assistance of Thomas J. Schlereth and Vincent P. DeSantis I selected sixteen Americans whom I believed personified the meaning of the spirit of '76 and its heritage in our nation's past. Someone else might have chosen differently. But I believe that these essays, written by uniquely competent scholars, capture the meaning and richness of the American tradition.

The essays initially appeared monthly in the *Elkhart Truth* beginning in March 1975 under the title " '76 That's the Spirit." But to make the project as lasting a contribution as possible, Mr. Decio decided to publish an edition of the collected essays and to present a copy of this book as a commemorative gift to the schools and libraries in the State of Indiana.

In organizing this project I had the cooperation of many people. William C. Malone, acting as liaison for Mr. Decio and the Commission, constantly prodded me throughout the past year, forcing me to substantiate my decisions. His assistant, Jane Woodruff, also aided the undertaking by her capable editorial assistance. Jeff Gillaspy and his staff at the *Elkhart Truth* competently guided the project through the press each month and published a product that won the plaudits of the public and the praise of the American Newspaper Publishers Association.

I also wish to express my gratitude for their cooperative spirit to the individual authors who contributed essays to the book. A note of thanks is also due to Philip Gleason, who first encouraged me to undertake this project.

A special acknowledgement of gratitude must be given to Arthur J. Decio, chairman of the Elkhart Bicentennial Commission. Without his belief in the value of such an endeavor and his generous support of it, the project would never have seen the light of day.

Jay P. Dolan
University of Notre Dame

HERITAGE OF '76

The Spirit and Heritage of 1776

JAY P. DOLAN

On July 2, 1776, a group of American patriots, acting as delegates to the Second Continental Congress, decided "that these United Colonies are, and, of right, ought to be free and independent states." Pledging themselves to the creation of a new nation, they voted to sever all political connection with Great Britain and abandon all allegiance to the British crown. One of the delegates, John Adams, in a letter to his wife, predicted that this momentous event "will be celebrated by succeeding generations as the great anniversary festival, a day of deliverance solemnized

3

with pomp and parade, with shows, games, sports, guns, bells, bonfires and illuminations, from one end of the continent to the other, from this time forward, forevermore."

Now, 200 years later, Americans are preparing for an anniversary celebration of their declaration of independence that John Adams would have found incredibly astonishing.

Since 1776 the United States has become a major nation in the international community, the thirteen colonies have increased to fifty states and the passage of time has witnessed the transformation of every aspect of American life. However momentous the events of July 1776 were to John Adams, they were only part of the first act of a great drama in the history of American civilization. Today, looking back over two hundred years of their history, Americans are seeking to recapture the spirit of '76. In the Bicentennial celebration the people of the United States are commemorating more than an event; we are celebrating a cause, a spirit that made the event possible, a spirit that inspired people to fight for freedom and to build a nation.

Long before the first drop of blood was shed at Lexington, a new spirit had been developing in the minds and hearts of the American people. It had not been present in 1750, but by 1776 it was placarded across buildings and signposts from Boston to Philadelphia. Town meetings proclaimed it in their assemblies, ballads celebrated it in song, and preachers announced it in the pulpits of the land. It was the spirit of freedom, the cause of liberty in the face of tyranny, that inspired Americans to declare their independence and to take up arms to preserve and protect the blessings of liberty. "Beardless boys," as one ballad portrayed them, "with hunting shirts and rifle guns" confronted the most powerful army in the world for the sake of their country and the cause of freedom.

This was the spirit that brought George Washington out of retirement and back to the battlefield to lead the nation to victory over the British. Thomas Paine celebrated it in his pamphlets as he reported the heroic struggles that took place during seven years of war.

When victory was won and peace was declared, a new nation was born. The United States had passed "from the tumult of war to the tranquillity of peace," wrote Thomas Paine, but the times that tried men's souls were not yet over. Unity had been forged in war, but the calm of peace threatened

4

to dissolve it. Then, for four months in 1787, the Founding Fathers argued, compromised, and finally agreed on a Constitution which, "will secure the blessings of liberty to ourselves and to our Posterity." Many of these men, patriots in war, had become architects of peace. Benjamin Rush, patriot, doctor, and scientist, sat in the midst of his comrades and reminded them that "there is nothing more common then to confuse the terms of the American Revolution with those of the late American War. The American War is over," he said, "but this is far from being the case with the American Revolution. On the contrary, nothing but the first act of the great drama is closed. It remains yet to establish and perfect our new form of government." The war for independence had unleashed the spirit of '76, but it was the task of the Constitutional Convention to codify it, put it in writing, and pass it on to future generations.

The Constitution assured that the blessings of liberty would be guaranteed and protected by a government responsible to the governed. To make this guarantee as explicit as possible, Congress adopted ten articles "in addition to, and amendment of, the Constitution of the United States of America." Commonly known as the Bill of Rights, these articles underlined the freedoms that Americans had fought to protect. They were the cornerstone of the democratic ideal emerging in American society. Included among these rights were the freedom of speech, of religion, of the press, as well as the right to a peaceful assembly, to due process of law, and to trial by jury. Indeed, not everyone was satisfied, and debate over the Constitution continues to our present day. Yet, it did consolidate the union and capture the spirit of democracy that Americans desired. Perhaps Benjamin Franklin expressed it best when he announced that he was voting for acceptance of the Constitution drafted by his colleagues "because I expect no better, and because I am not sure, that it is not the best."

The spirit of '76 lived on in the minds and hearts of the American people as the new, young nation began to expand its frontiers. In each generation men and women emerged who sought to uphold the ideal of freedom so that the blessings of liberty might endure as a living tradition. Isaac Backus, a Baptist minister from New England, took up the cause of religious freedom so that the sentiment of the law might become a living tradition. Years later, Henry David Thoreau in his essays and by his actions, reminded Americans of the dignity of the individual and the sacredness of the freedom of conscience. Harriet Tubman, a former slave known as the

"Moses of her people," waged a continuing crusade against slavery in her work with the Underground Railroad. Helen Hunt Jackson pricked the conscience of the nation in publicizing the century of dishonor that pillaged the American Indian. For these men and women the blessings of liberty were promised to all people regardless of their religion or the color of their skin. Their life and work wrote a new chapter in the ongoing history of the American Revolution as the spirit of '76 began to develop and adapt to a changing society.

During the course of American history the Supreme Court has presided over the development of the Constitution. Its chief responsibility was to see that the Constitution guaranteed what it promised. In the twentieth century Louis Brandeis distinguished himself as an advocate of the people and on the bench of the Supreme Court he sought to protect the individual liberties promised in the Bill of Rights. Martin Luther King, like Isaac Backus, was a Baptist minister, but the issue of his day was not religious freedom; it was racial freedom—the freedom to be black and share in the American dream. Harriet Tubman had worked to abolish slavery; Martin Luther King labored to abolish discrimination. Even though a century of time separated them, their work illustrated that the spirit of '76 was not a romantic sentiment of the past, but a living ideal challenging each generation of Americans.

The spirit of '76 not only launched an experiment in freedom, it also brought forth a new nation. Nurtured in the spirit of democracy and inspired by the contagion of liberty, America has sought to expand the achievements of the past in order to enrich the promises of the future.

The new nation was always in the process of further development; its geographical boundaries have continued to expand right up to the present generation. The ideal of democracy continually developed as the high standards of the past, proclaimed in the Declaration of Independence and preserved in the Constitution, inspired people to make this ideal intelligible and applicable to the machine age as well as the jet age. Science and technology helped to improve the quality of life. The buoyant optimism of the democratic ideal transformed education, making it free and accessible to all people. It appeared as if every aspect of life became enveloped in the democratic revolution as the spirit of '76 touched the imagination of each generation. Freedom from tyranny had given birth to freedom for democracy and every age wrote a new chapter in the continuing saga of the American Revolution.

In the nineteenth century the free enterprise system encouraged the rise of technology and the production of goods for the masses of society. The workingman could expect to find on his table such delicacies as fresh fish chowder and apple pie with some regularity, a luxury that even Thomas Jefferson did not enjoy. In 1876 Americans celebrated their first centennial anniversary and the magic of the machine captivated their attention. A few years later Thomas Edison lit up the business district of New York City with the flick of a switch; his genius for invention transformed night into day for millions of Americans. By making his inventions a product for the market, he gave a distinctive American cast to the idea of invention. Progress was to be enjoyed by the many, not coveted by the few.

John Dewey brought the same democratic spirit to education. As an educator his aim was growth for every citizen so that individuals would be more free. As one historian put it, "he made an America of the mind," and brought people new promise and new hope as well as new bewilderment. Frank Lloyd Wright took steel and concrete and formed a novel architectural style that blended in with the landscape of the American west. His design gave a distinctive imprint to American architecture. In architecture, science, and education—as well as in other areas of society—Americans manifested the ability of a free society to transcend the boundaries of the past and chart the course of the future. The contagion of freedom was always ready to unveil a new surprise.

The spirit of '76 is indeed multidimensional. It was born before the battle of Lexington and lived on long after the Constitutional Convention. In the following essays various scholars will probe the richness of this spirit that has enlivened the past 200 years of American history. They will examine the lives of outstanding Americans, some of whom have been mentioned above, and focus on their achievements in light of the spirit of '76. Our ancestors passed on to us a precious gift; we have labeled it the spirit of '76. That is the spirit that we celebrate on the anniversary of our independence.

To preserve the blessings of liberty and to fulfill the promises of democracy—that is the spirit of '76. That is the spirit that gave birth to this nation and sustained it during the past two centuries. The cause of freedom on behalf of democracy was a contagious spirit that spread across the landscape and transformed the nation. That was the real American Revolution. It began in 1776 and since then the challenge of every age has been to preserve the blessings of liberty and to fulfill the promises of democracy.

IN CONGRE

imous Declaration of the thi

When in the course of human events. it become necessary for. uth, the separate and equal station to which the Laws of Nature and of Na impel them to the separation. ——————— We hold these truth. that among these are Life. Liberty and the pursuit of Happiness. — verned. — That whenever any Form of Government becomes destructive of

Thomas Jefferson

MERRILL D. PETERSON

On the twenty-first day of June, 1775, a young, tall, red-headed Virginian with a beaming countenance took his seat in the Second Continental Congress at Philadelphia. His destiny lay before him, and a nation would rise with it. For six years, since he entered the House of Burgesses in Williamsburg, thirty-two-year-old Thomas Jefferson had been a leader in Virginia's resistance to the mother country. While not as prominent as Patrick Henry or Richard Henry Lee, he was of the same "radical" persua-

9

sion. Their talents were oratorical, and they would go down in history as the Demosthenes and Cicero of the American Revolution. Jefferson's talents were literary and philosophical. Drawing deeply from the fountains of knowledge, he had become perhaps the best educated Virginian of his generation. He was not only a practicing lawyer but a legal scholar, not only a wealthy planter but a scientist, architect, musician, linguist, and bibliophile.

It was as a draftsman of legislative papers and resolutions that he made his mark in Virginia. In 1774, during the crisis provoked by Parliament's Coercive Acts against Massachusetts, he wrote a 6,500-word paper intended as instructions for Virginia delegates to the First Continental Congress. Although deemed too bold for adoption in Williamsburg, his ardent young friends saw to its publication under the title, *A Summary View of the Rights of British America.* Jefferson, in lawyerlike fashion, drew his argument from the tradition of the English constitution, yet reached the startling conclusion that the Americans possessed the "natural right" of governing themselves. The logic of the argument pointed to independence. Neither Jefferson nor anyone else was ready for this leap in 1774, however. He stopped at the wholesale repudiation of Parliament's authority over the colonies—a position sufficiently radical in itself—which left allegiance to a common king the only bond of empire. Parliament being ruled out of the contest, the responsibility for reconciliation was placed on the shoulders of George III. Appropriately, the *Summary View* ended with an appeal to his justice, capped by a solemn warning: "No longer persevere in sacrificing the rights of one part of the empire to the inordinate desires of another; but deal out to all equal and impartial right. . . . The god who gave us life, gave us liberty at the same time; the hand of force may destroy, but cannot disjoin them. This, Sire, is our last, our determined resolution." Immediately republished in Philadelphia and London, the *Summary View* opened the final chapter in the polemics leading to the Revolution.

Jefferson's name had preceded him to Congress. He brought, as John Adams recalled, "a reputation for literature, science, and a happy talent for composition." His writings were known and admired for their "peculiar felicity of expression," and Adams noted with approval the judgment of a New York delegate that he was "the greatest rubber off of dust" to be met with in Congress—a gentleman of learning and science as well as a forthright politician. Just as he took his seat, news of the Battle of Bunker Hill reached the city. The war had begun in earnest. But resistance, not independence, was the watchword in 1775. Jefferson was at once asked to draft the momentous Declaration of the Causes and Necessity for Taking Up Arms. The moderate leader, John Dickinson of Pennsylvania, thought the paper unpardonably harsh and offensive to Great Britain. He was permitted to try his hand; and it was Dickinson's draft, incorporating large portions of Jefferson's that was adopted by Congress. Having already composed Virginia's reply to British Prime Minister Lord North's "conciliatory proposition," Jefferson performed the same service for Congress. This specious proposition, under which Parliament would forbear to tax the colonists, wholly misstated the grounds of opposition to Britain. It was held up to the world to deceive, Jefferson declared; but when the world came to reflect on the long chain of oppression, it would believe with the American patriots "that nothing but our own exertions may defeat the ministerial sentence of death or abject submission." He hoped through armed resistance to drive some sense into George III and force a reconciliation on terms compatible with American liberty. But as he wrote to a friend bound for London, rather than submit to Britain's pretensions to legislate for America he would "sink the whole island in the ocean."

The faint hope of reconciliation soon passed. Early in the new year, while Thomas Paine's *Common Sense* spread the doctrine of independence across the land and a revolutionary government took control in Virginia, Jefferson was detained at home by illness and family cares. Independence had made great strides when he returned to Congress on May 14. Some three weeks later Lee introduced the Virginia resolution declaring "that these United colonies are, & of right ought to be, free & independent states." After several days' debate, during which the moderates of the middle colonies pleaded for more time, it was agreed to postpone decision on the motion until July 1. Meanwhile, a committee was appointed to prepare a declaration of independence. Jefferson found himself named at the head of this committee of five: Benjamin Franklin and John Adams, both decidedly his seniors in age and service, Roger Sherman of Connecticut, Robert R. Livingston of New York, and himself. The committee met and, on Jefferson's testimony, he agreed to write the draft. Years later Adams had a different recollection. He recalled a conversation which began with Jefferson asking him to do the honors.

11

"Oh! no."

"Why will you not? You ought to do it."

"I will not."

"Why?"

"Reasons enough."

"What can be your reasons?"

"Reason first—You are a Virginian, and a Virginian ought to appear at the head of this business. Reason second—I am suspected, obnoxious, and unpopular. You are very much otherwise. Reason third—You can write ten times better than I can."

"Well, if you are decided I will do as well as I can."

Even if the conversation never occurred, it is suggestive of why Jefferson became the author of the Declaration of Independence.

In his lodgings on the second floor of bricklayer Joseph Graff's home at Seventh and Market (now High) Street, before and after daily meetings of Congress, Jefferson composed this most famous of American state papers. How many false starts, how many drafts he may have made on the way to the so-called "rough draft" cannot be known for certain, but, this finished, he submitted it to Adams and Franklin for correction. "Their alterations were one or two only, merely verbal," Jefferson later said. He then went through the draft again, introducing many verbal changes and several additions of his own. Satisfied now, he sat down with a little portable writing desk built to his design by a previous landlord, and penned the fair copy of the Declaration.

At no time, he later said, did he turn to book or pamphlet or writing of any kind. This was not strictly accurate. The indictment against the King—eighteen incisively paragraphed charges, authenticated in the historical record, and artfully exhibited as *prima facie* proof of the King's design to reduce the Americans under "absolute despotism"—was drawn from the preamble of the constitution he had himself drafted for Virginia. Of course, the indictment ran against the King because Congress had already repudiated the authority of Parliament. It seems likely, too, that the Virginia Declaration of Rights, the work of George Mason, influenced the phrasing of Jefferson's philosophical second paragraph. Nevertheless, his statement was faithful to the spirit of the work as he understood it:

12

Not to find out new principles, or new arguments, never before thought of, not merely to say things which had never been said before; but to place before mankind the common sense of the subject, and to justify ourselves in the independent stand we are compelled to take. Neither aiming at originality of principle or sentiment, nor yet copied from any particular or previous writing, it was intended to be an expression of the American mind, and to give to that expression the proper tone and spirit called for by the occasion.

The full committee, after making a number of verbal alterations, reported the proposed Declaration of Independence to Congress on June 28. It was received, heard, and laid on the table pending adoption—a foregone conclusion—of Lee's resolution, which occurred on July 2. Congress then debated the Declaration line by line for two and one-half days. The philosophical preamble was quickly approved, but many changes, mostly stylistic, some of substance, were made in the body and conclusion of the work. Jefferson squirmed under this ordeal. He was especially incensed by the elimination of the longest, angriest, and climactic count against the King: "waging cruel war against human nature itself" by imposing on the colonies the traffic in African slaves. Jefferson said it was struck at the behest of South Carolina and Georgia, bent on continuing the slave trade. Perhaps. But it ill became the Americans who had profited from this infernal traffic to lay the whole blame on George III. The charge did not ring true, which was the better reason for striking it. Like many authors before and since, Jefferson thought his original was superior to the final product. He was wrong. The Declaration of Independence emerged from Congress on July Fourth a stronger document, yet with the stamp of Jefferson's genius indelibly upon it.

In a document of under 1,500 words, Jefferson not only set forth the grievances of the colonies which justified their independence but advanced in axiomatic terms a revolutionary philosophy for the new nation. Without this the independence of the Americans—three million people along the western Atlantic frontier of Europe—would scarcely have been an epochal event in human history. As it was, the colonial revolt—the first great colonial revolt of the modern era—opened an age of democratic revolution in the Western world. What were these "self-evident truths" of the Declaration?

First, "all men are created equal." Not in native abilities or in worldly rewards but in the order of nature and in fundamental rights.

Second, "they are endowed . . . with certain unalienable Rights . . . among these are Life, Liberty, and the pursuit of Happiness." These rights being *natural* are antecedent to government; indeed, the whole object of government is to secure individuals in them. The usual formulation was "life, liberty, and property." By substituting for the latter "the pursuit of happiness," Jefferson altered the hierarchy of human values.

Third, "Governments derive . . . their just powers from the consent of the governed." Always before in history ultimate authority had been embodied in the governing power; the theory of the Declaration placed it in the people, thereby subordinating the rulers to the ruled.

Fourth, "whenever . . . Government becomes destructive to these ends, it is the Right of the People to alter or abolish it, and to institute new government." The very right that brought the nation into being was thus built into its foundation.

In the Declaration of Independence, a philosophy of liberty and self-government was symbolized forever in words that inspired action. The Americans had a war to win, a continent to unite, if they were to make good their claim to independence; but they also had the greater task of implementing the revolutionary creed Jefferson had given them in the life and institutions of the new nation. This was not the work of a year, a decade, even a generation; in fact, it could never be finished. Abraham Lincoln, on the eve of the Civil War, liked to recall the principles that had presided over America's birth. They had made the Revolution—more than a mere separation from the motherland—an ongoing commitment to the freedom and equality of all men.

> All honor to Jefferson, to the man who, in the concrete pressure of a struggle for national independence . . . had the coolness, forecast, and capacity to introduce into a merely revolutionary document, an abstract truth, and so to embalm it there, that today, and in all coming days, it shall be a rebuke and a stumbling block to the very harbingers of re-appearing tyranny and oppression.

Now, on the nation's Bicentennial, the words of the Declaration have been worn thin by time and grown stale in our throats. Yet they are still at the heart of the American ideal. And the challenge at the beginning of the third century is to see that the ideal works, not on the terms of Jefferson's day, or of Lincoln's, but of ours.

The *American* Crisis.

Number I.

By the Author of Common Sense.

THESE are the times that try men's souls: The summer soldier and the sunshine patriot will, in this crisis, shrink from the service of his country; but he that stands it NOW, deserves the love and thanks of man and woman. Tyranny, like hell, is not easily conquered; yet we have this consolation with us, that the harder the conflict, the more glorious the triumph. What we obtain too cheap, we esteem too lightly :---'Tis dearness only that gives every thing its value. Heaven knows how to set a proper price upon its goods; and it would be strange indeed, if so celestial an article as FREEDOM should not be highly rated. Britain, with an army to enforce her tyranny, has declared, that she has a right (*not only to* TAX, but) "*to* " BIND *us in* ALL CASES WHATSOEVER," and if being *bound in that manner* is not slavery, then is there not such a thing as slavery upon earth. Even the expression is impious, for so unlimited a power can belong only to GOD.

Thomas Paine

A. OWEN ALDRIDGE

The first public call for American independence came from a newly arrived Englishman, Thomas Paine, who devoted his literary genius to keeping the morale of American soldiers and civilians high throughout the dark and difficult months of the revolutionary war. Born in Thetford in 1737, Paine followed the trades of corset-maker, schoolmaster, itinerant preacher, and customs inspector before making the acquaintance of Benjamin Franklin, who was then in England as an agent for the colony of

Pennsylvania. Recognizing in Paine a kindred spirit, Franklin persuaded him to emigrate to Philadelphia. Almost as soon as he landed in November 1774, the country was "set on fire about his ears" by the demands of the colonists for relaxation of oppressive restrictions and taxes. Paine not only dared to advocate independence as the only workable solution, but had the courage and foresight to prescribe a representative system of government as an improvement over hereditary monarchy and hereditary aristocracy. Paine's stirring pamphlet *Common Sense,* published January 9, 1776, instantly changed the sentiments of a majority of the colonists from indecision to patriotic fervor. Paine closed the period of debate and hesitation.

Within three months, over 100,000 copies of his pamphlet were sold, a number equivalent to nearly seven million in proportion to the present population of the United States. Paine donated all his profits to buy mittens for the troops then marching off to battle in Quebec. In *Common Sense,* Paine was the first to call for a declaration of independence and for a constitutional convention, and he was the first to refer to the Free and Independent States of America.

"A government of our own is our natural right," Paine declared, specifying a system which guarantees freedom and property to all men. For Paine, the greatest task of government was to safeguard the free exercise of religion. "The King of America," he proclaimed, "reigns above." Although not neglecting arguments based on self interest, Paine insisted that it was the duty of the colonists to all mankind as well as to themselves which required them to renounce their connection with Britain. He vindicated independence as a moral obligation before taking up the question of how it could be brought about. Many of his principles are valid today.

To those who argued that the economic survival of the colonies depended on the strength and protection of the British empire, Paine replied that American raw materials had been drained to support British arms around the world. Challenging the advocates of reconciliation to point to a single advantage which the colonies enjoyed through their connection with Britain, he argued that their welfare lay in casting off all trade restrictions and opening commerce to all of Europe. This they could do only by going their own way.

Paine put down the "much boasted" British constitution as "imperfect, subject to convulsions and incapable of producing what it seems to promise." He demonstrated that the king and Parliament were equally guilty of "a grievous oppression of the American people." By arguing that British policy aspired to the complete confiscation of American property, Paine persuaded his readers that no other solution was acceptable but complete separation from Britain. The policies of the empire, he charged, had embroiled the colonies in a series of armed conflicts in which they had no interest and no stake. In order to leave a heritage of peace to their children, they were obliged to resist the tyranny which oppressed them at home and produced wars in foreign lands.

Perhaps even more important than Paine's advocacy of independence itself was his insistence upon unity. If the colonies failed to work together, he maintained, they could never resist British arms nor establish a workable government. Their strength was continental, not local or provincial, Paine insisted, and it lay in cooperation, not in numbers. Paine's vision extended even beyond the American continent. Rejecting the argument that Americans were bound to England by racial ties, he claimed brotherhood instead with every European Christian. Freedom, according to Paine, had been hunted round the globe but had found refuge in America. Because it now belonged to the colonists, they disdained submission.

Paine considered the struggle to maintain liberty in America as identical with the cause of all mankind. He prided himself on taking "nature for his guide" and assumed that since all men of reason would do likewise, his arguments would be heeded. The tie with Britain, he affirmed, had to be broken because the precepts of empire lead to the "general massacre of mankind." Paine condemned Tories who supported British rule as apostates "from the order of mankind." In Paine's thought society is based upon the common interest and the universal rights of nature. In concrete terms, "Of more worth is one honest man to society and in the sight of God, than all the crowned ruffians that ever lived." The only voices Paine would recognize were "those of a good citizen, an open and resolute friend, and a virtuous supporter of the rights of mankind and of the free and independent states of America."

In retrospect, Paine observed that the independence of America would have come about at some time or another—even without Lexington and Concord or without *Common Sense*. What was important in Paine's opinion is that the breaking away as it actually took place in 1776 represented a philosophical movement. "It was the opportunity of *beginning the world anew,* as it were; and of bringing forward a *new system* of government in which the rights of all men should be preserved that gave *value* to independence."

Through his pamphlet, Paine succeeded in rallying support for a new nation; but this was not enough to bring about victory. Before his dream could be realized, a war had to be fought, an army had to be equipped and regularly provisioned, and money had to be raised to pay for ammunition and supplies. All of this required that the morale of the people be kept high and their support of the Continental Congress firm. Throughout the struggle, Paine published a series of commentaries on military and diplomatic affairs, designed to unite the American people in their determination to achieve victory. Called *American Crisis,* these papers were appropriately issued in thirteen segments, the number of states in the new nation.

Paine himself enlisted in the militia of Pennsylvania, and in the months immediately after the Declaration of Independence saw action at Fort Lee in New Jersey. In these days, which he later called the "black times of '76," the campaign went badly for the American troops. Washington was forced to retreat from New York all the way across New Jersey. Eleven days after the American general crossed to the Pennsylvania shores of the Delaware River, with an army decimated by the expiring of enlistments, Paine published the first number of the *Crisis.* Its opening lines have become justly famous: "These are the times that try men's souls: The summer soldier and the sunshine patriot will, in this crisis, shrink from the service of his country, but he that stands it NOW, deserves the love and thanks of man and woman."

No other literary work summarizes the spirit of the American Revolution as sharply and as fully as does the *Crisis.* The ideals, expectations, sacrifices and daily concerns of the people are set forth in ringing phrases. As in his opening lines, Paine stresses the duty of every citizen, the rich and poor, the farmer and the city dweller, and he scorns as dead "the heart that feels not now." In contrast to these dead souls, he praises the inhabitants of the middle states who nobly did their duty in supporting Washington's troops during this retreat. "They were witnesses to the almost expiring flame of human freedom." Towards the end of the war he explained American persistence by the operation of their natural feelings. The colonists had displayed bravery in distress, and serenity in conquest, and had called upon "every passion, but that of despair." It was, moreover, "the humanity of America" which kept her from indulging in acts of retaliation against the cruelty and rapaciousness of the British.

Emphasizing the popular foundation of the Revolution, Paine affirmed that its enterprises and active measures were being pursued by all ranks of men. "The cause of America stands not on the will of a few, but on the broad foundation of property and popularity." Its suffering people, he says, motivated by the good of all, have wagered their all on the outcome. As in *Common Sense,* Paine stresses the universal significance of the struggle. It is the first in which the destiny of an entire continent depends, and it is the first to give man an opportunity of setting an example of peace to the whole world. Speaking in his own character, Paine declares that his principles are universal and that his "attachment is to all the world." As a writer, he speaks for all mankind.

In a further doctrine taken over from *Common Sense,* Paine contends that the indispensable ingredient for military and political success is the union of the states, "the great hinge" on which the whole machine turns, and the foundation of American national character.

Although in later life Paine published a theological work which has been considered by unfriendly critics as an attack upon religion, *The Age of Reason* (1796), this work was actually written as an attempt to check the growing tendency of the French Revolution toward atheism. It is a powerful statement of the philosophy of deism or, as it was called in the eighteenth century, the religion of nature. Paine, throughout his entire life, was a confirmed believer in divine providence. In the *Crisis,* therefore, he maintains that the eventual victory of America is divinely appointed. He more than once indicates his belief that God is in control of the government of the world, and he considers freedom as a "celestial article." In his opinion, it is the will of God which had separated England and America, and "the deed is registered for eternity." He has no doubt that America will flourish, "the favorite of Heaven and the friend of mankind." From a purely worldly perspective, moreover, the Americans have a righteous cause, fighting as they are, "not to enslave, but to make a country free."

Looking back upon the conflict in his last *Crisis,* when "the times that tried men's souls" were finally at an end, Paine confidently affirms that the American Revolution has done more "to enlighten the world, and diffuse a spirit of freedom and liberality among mankind" than any previous event in the history of human affairs. In taking leave of his fellow-countrymen, he admits that he will always feel an honest pride in the part he has "taken and acted, and a gratitude to Nature and Providence" for giving him the opportunity "to be of some use to mankind."

Paine wrote the thirteen numbers of the *Crisis* primarily to bolster internal morale, but he also had an eye to public opinion in Europe, particularly in France, which became an ally of the American insurgents in 1778. An influential French writer, the Abbé Raynal, had charged in a history of the American Revolution that the conflict had no moral foundation; it merely concerned the right of the mother country to tax its colonies. Since Paine's *Common Sense* had attempted to prove that the American conflict represented a revolution in philosophy as well as in statecraft, he lost no time in replying to the French historian, publishing in 1782 a book-length *Letter to the Abbé Raynal,* devoted to "the well enlightened field of philosophical reflection." Here he portrays the American Revolution as a giant step in the history of social progress, illustrating "a greater fitness in mankind to extend and complete the civilization of nations."

When a social revolution on this order eventually broke out in France, Paine defended it in another book, his *Rights of Man* (1791–1792), using the same general principles which he had first propounded in *Common Sense.* Invited to France by leading patriots, he lived there for ten years and was twice a member of the supreme legislative body of the nation, a distinction never accorded to him in America. In his old age, he returned to the United States to become, before his death in 1809, a disillusioned spectator of the party struggles between Federalists and Democrats. He contributed several essays to newspapers, signing himself among other pseudonyms "An Old Friend of 76" and "A Spark from the Spirit of 76." His proudest achievement remained his service to the Revolution, and in his will he asked to have a head stone engraved with his name, age, and the words "author of *Common Sense.*"

Exselene
georg
general
Waschingd

TO ALL BRAVE, HEALTHY, ABLE BODIED, AND WELL
DISPOSED YOUNG MEN,
IN THIS NEIGHBOURHOOD, WHO HAVE ANY INCLINATION TO JOIN THE TROOPS,
NOW RAISING UNDER
GENERAL WASHINGTON,
FOR THE DEFENCE OF THE
LIBERTIES AND INDEPENDENCE
OF THE UNITED STATES,
Against the hostile designs of foreign enemies,

TAKE NOTICE,

George Washington

MARSHALL SMELSER

The Continental Army of the United States had kept the bored British Army cooped in Boston through the winter of 1775–1776. When spring came each side decided to attack the other. The Americans were quicker.

On a chilly and windy night in mid-March of 1776, Major General George Washington, tall, strongly muscled and big boned, walked his horse to the top of a hill on Boston's south side where he had his men dig trenches and set up stone-filled barrels to roll downhill against any clambering enemy. They then mounted cannon which the former book seller and present chief of artillery, fat Henry Knox, had sledded during the winter from captured Fort Ticonderoga. These guns began to boom to cover the noise of the digging. When daylight came, the watching commander, tall in his saddle, had a position from which his artillery could flatten Boston if he said the word. The British could see it too, and gave up without resistance, sailing away from Boston on St. Patrick's Day.

Son of a family which had lived in Virginia for generations, young George Washington had been a surveyor of wild lands. Life in the wilderness made him a good horseman and woodsman. In the French and Indian War he commanded the Virginia troops and was at Braddock's bloody defeat in 1755. When things quieted down he married the richest woman in America, Martha Dandridge, widow of Daniel Custis.

Washington had inherited Mount Vernon from his half-brother in 1752. From 1759 to 1774 he lived the life of a country gentleman. He represented his neighbors in the House of Burgesses for fifteen years, getting experience as a practical politician which was to be very useful in later and more stirring times.

All through these years George Washington was a leader of the local aristocrats who accepted King George III as their king, but who ran the internal affairs of Virginia as they saw fit. But times were changing. In Britain it seemed that the Americans were getting the benefits of empire without its responsibilities and the empire need reorganizing. The Parliament passed law after law more closely regulating the lives of white colonial Americans—customs taxes, laws regulating money, even the Stamp Act, an internal revenue tax which was something unheard of in the relations of the parts of the empire. To judge by the Virginia newspapers of the time, the king and the Parliament lost popularity steadily.

The men with whom George Washington governed Virginia were big men in Virginia. They put up with no hindrance from lesser folk at home (little was offered) and they were not minded to take orders from men across the ocean who claimed to be greater.

When the Bostonians showed the same spirit in the Boston Tea Party (1773) and felt the punishment of the British Parliament, which closed their port until they paid for the ruined tea, the native ruling groups in most of the colonies met in Philadelphia in the First Continental Congress (1774) to let the king know, in respectful language, that they did not like the steady growth of British interference in colonial affairs. The Virginia House of Burgesses elected seven delegates to the congress and showed its regard for Washington by giving him the second highest vote-total.

George Washington, aged forty-two, was in his physical prime. Surveyor, soldier, farmer, and politician, he was, at the moment, also the richest man in the thirteen angry colonies. Of native-born Americans young enough to serve, he had the most experience of military command. No younger man in the southern colonies was more valued for reliability.

The First Continental Congress met in Philadelphia for seven weeks in the fall of 1774. This intercolonial congress was very important for making the protesters of America personally acquainted with each other, and leaders from all colonies were happily surprised to find so much agreement in other colonies. In drafting the respectful complaints to the British government, George Washington took no leading part; but he impressed the northern delegates as a man of solid sense. When the delegates forwarded their complaints to Britain they adjourned, agreeing to meet again in May 1775, if their grievances had not been met.

By the following May things had gone from bad to very much worse. In April blood had flowed, war had started, and the British army was besieged in Boston by 13,000 angered but poorly organized Yankees. When he heard that war had started, George Washington said he was willing to raise and take a regiment to Boston at his own expense.

In June 1775 the Second Continental Congress adopted the Yankee volunteers as a national army. To make it a truly continental force, the Congress chose generals from all the colonies. For its commander in chief they chose that most experienced, most determined, most eligible Virginian, George Washington.

Washington was in Massachusetts during the winter of 1775–1776 to put the army into shape. With firm training, careful selection of officers, a naval blockade of Boston, and the collection of supplies, he had made a useful force by the spring of 1776.

The seizure of the heights south of Boston in March 1776 was the fruit of that winter's hard work. Washington had outfoxed the British. Their evacuation of the city, a bloodless success, was his first victory in the War for Independence. He was now a general with a winning record.

The British land forces in America had received a new commander, Sir William Howe, during the siege of Boston. After leaving Boston he was superbly reinforced by a large expeditionary force and sailed to attack New York. This was a new situation for Washington. It was one thing to besiege an enemy in a town; it was quite another to defend a town.

Washington's mind was slow. His defense of New York in the summer of 1776—the summer of the Declaration of Independence—was confused. Not yet skilled in handling large forces, he divided his troops in a shortsighted effort to be strong everywhere at once. In the main fight, the battle of Long Island (August 27), Washington unwisely risked his whole army, one might even say the whole cause of independence, and escaped only by luck of the weather. In two months the more professional Howe then cleared the rebel army from New York in a series of short sharp battles that cost the Continentals nearly five thousand men and, perhaps worse, nearly all of the American military supplies. Washington had been soundly beaten. But the baronial Virginian did not even think of yielding to an English knight.

With a remnant of a beaten army, Washington retreated across New Jersey in glorious fall weather, losing deserters every day and followed lazily by the confident British. It was a gloomy time for rebels, and Washington was depressed. When he crossed into Pennsylvania he wrote to a relative that he must get new troops or "the game is pretty near up." There were bleak days ahead, to be sure, but this was his darkest hour.

And now he showed that stubbornness could be a match for professionalism. With the remnant of an army he turned like a cornered lion, beat his foe at Trenton by surprise, and carried on the war for six more years, completely devoted to a cause that in future years often seemed nearly as hopeless as during that miserable fall of 1776. He never gave up; he always stubbornly pressed for independence. Pretended superiors in Britain were determined to govern America; he was determined they would not. In the end his cause won. With his rocklike character he contributed more than any other one person.

28

After the final satisfying victory at Yorktown in 1781, when Cornwallis's redcoats marched with reversed muskets to surrender while their band played "The World Turned Upside Down," and after news of the Treaty with King George III which legalized American independence, Washington went home to Mount Vernon.

While the army was disbanding, Colonel Lewis Nicola hinted that Washington could be king. He spurned it, thus preserving the republic, for if *he* wished no crown the people would make no other man king.

Because of wartime neglect, Washington's farm needed attention. He studied the newest discoveries in crop rotation and fertilizers. The letters he wrote show his zest for farming. The letters he received show he was thought of as a hero, both in America and Europe.

But the job of making America a working republic was incomplete. The states cooperated poorly, interstate commerce was hampered, foreign nations had little respect for America, and the union was not strong enough to govern. Some men had known that a stronger union was needed. Washington, for one, believed that too much emphasis on states' rights had kept his army underfed and short of weapons.

In 1786 revolutionary leaders were shocked when desperate debtors in Massachusetts rose up in Shays's Rebellion and had to be dispersed by force. Leaders of the struggle for independence feared the republic might die young. Wrote Washington (August 1, 1786):

> I do not conceive we can exist long as a nation without having lodged somewhere a power which will pervade the whole Union in as energetic a manner as the authority of the State governments extends over the several states.

Moved by such views (other influential men thought the same) the feeble congress called a meeting at Philadelphia in 1787 to correct the weaknesses of the United States.

One of the wisest decisions of the Constitutional Convention was its choice of Washington as presiding officer. Because the Convention met behind closed doors there might have been suspicion of a subversive plot, but the public was sure that Washington would not help to throw out what the Revolution gained.

29

The Convention was a caucus of seasoned politicians who drew up a government as strongly centralized as people would accept. Once they created the office of president they were reasonably sure that Washington would be the man, hence they made it a rather more powerful office than otherwise. And the fact that Washington was a coauthor helped to get the Constitution ratified.

The Electoral College twice unanimously chose Washington to be president of the United States. Despite his modest disclaimers we know he was pleased to have gained the highest rank open to an American. His presidency was not always serene, but it was always prudent. Like all presidents he found that journalists could be painful, but he did no more against critics than to use a little strong language in private. Washington carefully presided over precedent-setting domestic policies, enforced federal law, and steered the country peacefully through the period of the wars of the French Revolution. When he declined a third term he left a federal administration that worked well. If it had failed he would get the blame. We must give him the credit.

American independence was not gained by Washington alone, but no other person contributed as much to the cause. He was steadfast during setbacks. His political experience helped him to get along with the civilian leaders of the Continental and Federal Congresses. No one was more energetic and stubborn in the long labors to separate the British colonies from the British kingdom, and to found a workable republic. The Continental Army got its perseverance from him. He was not a very lovable man, but he had more important qualities, he was trustworthy, prudent, determined.

What was he fighting for? Some of his colleagues said they rebelled for abstract legal and philosophical reasons. But George Washington fought for a practical cause: to stop the newfangled broadening of British powers in America. His aim was to keep the right of free Americans to run their local affairs as they had for generations. That was his understanding of the spirit of 1776.

Benjamin Rush

THOMAS J. SCHLERETH

"The American war is over; but this is far from being the case with the American revolution. On the contrary, nothing but the first act of the great drama is closed. It remains yet to establish and perfect our new forms of government...." So spoke Dr. Benjamin Rush to his fellow Philadelphians as they celebrated the Fourth of July in 1787. Eleven summers before, Rush, the only medical doctor to sign the Declaration of Independence, had been a part of the revolutionary movement. Signing the

33

rebellious document was to him, however, only a beginning. Rush under-stood the Revolution to be more than a mere act of political separation; it was "a new moral force unleashed in the world," an historical precedent destined to achieve nothing less than "the universal social redemption of mankind." Stirred by his personal involvement in "the republican ferment" of 1776, Rush charged his generation to extend the revolutionary spirit to reform American society.

Rush was a reformer by birthright. Born in 1746 near Philadelphia, Benjamin was descended from John Rush who had fought in the Puritan Revolution under Oliver Cromwell. When Rush's father died young, pre-cocious Benjamin was raised by his mother, who, recognizing his talent, sent him to West Nottingham Academy (Maryland) and the College of New Jersey (later Princeton). Apt at composition and oratory, Rush first considered a career in law but eventually decided on medicine. In 1761 he apprenticed himself to an established Philadelphia physician and also began attending lectures at the College of Philadelphia (later the University of Pennsylvania). Notwithstanding his medical studies, Rush closely followed the political agitation surrounding the Stamp Act of 1765. During this crisis, the nineteen-year-old student invoked "good Old Oliver Cromwell's spirit" in urging Philadelphians to resist the British Parliament. Approving of the public protests that hanged stamp officers in effigy, he supported passage of nonimportation agreements among the colonies.

Parliament repealed the Stamp Act the following year and that summer Rush left for further medical study at the University of Edinburgh. In the Scottish capital, he learned the latest medical theories from William Cullen, an outstanding diagnostician, and Joseph Black, chemist and dis-coverer of carbon dioxide. Others nurtured his growing republicanism: John Wilkes, the parliamentary agitator; Catherine Macaulay, the Whig histo-rian; and Benjamin Franklin, surrogate father for all young American innocents abroad. Rush came home to Pennsylvania in 1769 a doctor of medicine and a political radical.

Immediately he set up practice in Philadelphia. He also joined the faculty at the College of Philadelphia and the adjacent Pennsylvania Hospi-tal, where, at twenty-three, he assumed the first professorship of chemistry in the colonies. His *Syllabus of A Course of Lectures on Chemistry* (1770) became the first American chemistry textbook.

Politics continued to concern young Rush. When the First Continental Congress met in September 1774, he hobnobbed with John and Sam Adams, entertaining them and George Washington at his Walnut Street home. Quick to recognize that the war effort would require domestic support, he organized a joint-stock company to promote the home industries of woolen, cotton, and linen manufacturing to counter the British embargo.

After a chance meeting with the newly arrived Thomas Paine in Robert Aitken's bookshop in February 1775, Rush made the fateful suggestion that Paine write a polemic urging American independence rather than reconciliation with Britain. Paine set to work, discussing his early drafts with Rush, and considered calling the now famous pamphlet "Plain Truth." Rush, however, proposed the title "Common Sense." He also sought out a sympathetic printer, saw the tract through its publication on January 10, 1776, just a day before going off to marry Julia Stockton, daughter of the New Jersey revolutionary, Richard Stockton. Even if he had done nothing more for the patriot cause, the literary promotion of Paine's stirring work would have been ample service to the independence movement.

1776 was a heady year for Rush. In addition to his marriage and his support of Paine's writing, he was elected a member of the Provincial Conference which called the convention to frame Pennsylvania's first state constitution, and in July he was also chosen to represent his state in the Continental Congress. Rush served nine months in the Congress concerning himself principally with securing medical supplies and provisions for the war effort. His most memorable act—a ritual he always recalled as of the utmost moment in his life—was adding his signature to the great Declaration. Unlike any of his fellow rebels, Rush was the only man who signed the document along with his father-in-law.

After his term in the Congress expired, Rush accepted a commission as a surgeon general in the Army of the Middle Department. As a volunteer physician, he had already aided Washington's troops at the battles of Trenton and Princeton. During his stormy tenure in the medical corps, he attempted to prevent smallpox by urging the innoculation of all troops and campaigned incessantly for changes in the conditions and administration of military hospitals. In the decade after the war, he exerted his influence to reform the Articles of Confederation and vigorously urged the Pennsylvania convention, of which he was a member, to ratify the new federal Constitution.

Returning to his private practice and his teaching career, Rush remained convinced that the Revolution signaled more than a political transfer of power. "We have changed our forms of government," he wrote fellow reformer Richard Price in 1786, "but it remains yet to effect a revolution in our principles, opinions, and manners so as to accommodate them to the forms of government we have adopted." Rush spent the rest of his life agitating, speaking, and writing to effect such a cultural revolution in America.

He first set about infusing republican principles into the fledgling American medical profession. In writings such as *Observations Upon the Duties of A Physician* and his lectures to the 3,000 students he taught over forty years, Rush insisted that a doctor's responsibilities to his fellow citizens were civil as well as medical. The "republican physician," Rush told his colleagues, should expose fraud in his profession, donate his services freely, and work to protect the medically incapacitated, the widowed and the orphaned. He sought the democratization of American medicine by refusing to use antiquated medical jargon in discussing a patient's illness; he wrote prescriptions in English rather than the traditional Latin, so that his clients knew the nature of their medicines. He was not above prescribing and consulting by mail or in the newspapers: he believed that in a revolutionary age and a republican nation, medicine, like government, should be purged of mystery and thereby made plain to every citizen.

In his efforts to render medicine as egalitarian as politics, Rush attempted to reform and increase the country's hospitals. Almost half the soldiers who had died in the Revolutionary War, he maintained, lost their lives because of the inadequacies of the military hospitals. Civilian lives continued to be wasted. To remedy this Rush established, in 1786, the Philadelphia Dispensary—the first free, medical clinic in the nation. He urged that such public clinics, open to all citizens, be established by every municipal government.

In no instance was Rush's promotion of increased hospital care more revolutionary than in his work with the mentally ill. Beginning in 1783 when he first joined the staff of the Pennsylvania Hospital, Rush studied mental disease with a profound dedication. After 1810, his relationship to the hospital's mental patients became painfully personal when he had to commit his eldest son. Rush wrote treatises, pamphlets, even newspaper articles to press the case for humane and judicious treatment of the insane. His reforms included removal of the mentally ill from criminal prisons, their placement in sanitary hospitals staffed by specialists, and occupational therapy to rehabilitate them for their return to society. After thirty years of research he completed *Medical Inquiries and Observation Upon the Diseases of the Mind* (1812). A remarkable work, now dated, it was an enlightened and pioneering study that anticipated the approach of modern psychiatry.

If sometimes dogmatic—for example in his uncompromising therapeutics of bloodletting and purging—Rush often showed courage in opposing the prejudices of the medical profession and the lay public. His hypothesis that the yellow-fever epidemic of 1793 was caused partly by poor sanitation shocked smug Philadelphians and he was ostracized. Rush risked his life that year by remaining in the city to help the dying and to study the disease. He pioneered in relating dentistry to physiology, urged Americans to partake of more natural foods and exercise (including jogging and golf), and helped establish veterinary medicine in the U.S. Under his leadership Philadelphia became the center of medical education on this continent.

The intellectual pursuits of Benjamin Rush went beyond his medical practice and research. A deep personal sense of civic duty led him to bring his talents to bear on numerous public problems. Nearly every Philadelphia philosophical, philanthropic, religious or reform organization counted him on its rolls, in many cases, among their charter members or officers. Civic consciousness was a concrete expression of a conviction Rush espoused for every citizen of the Republic: "Every man is public property. His time and talents—his youth, his old age—nay, more, his life, his all belong to his country."

In one sense Rush had begun his reform of America even before Lexington. In 1773 he wrote his first attack against slavery, arguing that as the colonists wished liberty from their British overlords, so too, slaves deserved freedom from their American masters. To implement such a belief and to muster an intercolonial movement against the slave trade, Rush, along with other Philadelphians, founded the Pennsylvania Society for Promoting the Abolition of Slavery in 1774. As a member of this first antislavery society in America, Rush took an energetic role in its campaigns, becoming its president in 1803 and serving in that office until his death.

As a member of another reform group, the Society for Promoting Political Enquiries, Rush read a paper at Franklin's home in 1787 outlining his proposals for prison reform. This treatise, one of the earliest American studies in penology, pointed out that most punishments were unduly severe, the death penalty was invoked for minor crimes, and no attempts were ever made to probe the psychology of criminal behavior or to rehabilitate the felon. Rush demanded that a republican society eliminate the pillory, stocks, and whipping post as artifacts of autocratic regimes. Prisons should be built as hospitals wherein "the criminally diseased" could be cured. Capital punishment had no place in a democratic state where every human life was significant. In 1794, largely due to Rush's efforts, Pennsylvania revised its criminal code with the death penalty reserved for deliberate homicide only.

In addition to outlawing public and capital punishments, the reformer hoped also to rid the Republic of dueling, militarism, and even war itself. An early advocate of limited gun control, his idealistic pacifism prompted him to propose that a secretary of peace be appointed in the federal cabinet to balance the proclivities of the already established secretary of war.

Many American revolutionaries, such as Franklin, Jefferson and Madison, saw their legacy extending principally through an educated electorate. No republic, insisted Jefferson, could be ignorant and free. Rush likewise claimed "without learning, men are incapable of knowing their rights, and where learning is confirmed to a few people, liberty can be neither equal nor universal." He realized that "the business of education has acquired a new complexion by the independence of our country," and therefore wrote his *Thoughts Upon the Mode of Education Proper in A Republic* (1786). Rush would have implemented his educational reforms in a plan almost identical to Jefferson's proposals for Virginia in 1778. Universal, free, public instruction would be available in tax-supported schools at the township level. Students would then proceed to four-year colleges (really academies) regionally distributed in each state. The colleges, in turn, would feed their best students into a university located in the state capital. Rush, who anticipated colleges to be "absolutely necessary to preserve liberty in the state" and the "best bulwarks of the blessings obtained by the Revolution," was a founder, fund raiser, and faculty recruiter for Dickinson College in 1781.

He also proposed that a federal, postgraduate university be created in the national capital. Here government and public service would be taught to students from every state. "We require certain qualifications in lawyers, physicians, and clergymen," he explained, "why therefore should we commit our country to men who cannot produce vouchers of their qualifications for this important trust?" Rush, who supported state regulation of the professions to eliminate charlatans, asked "why should we not be restrained in like manner, by law, from employing quacks in government?"

By upgrading public office through education, Benjamin Rush, more than most other public men of his day, endeavored to expand educational facilities for American women. A founder of the Young Ladies Academy of Philadelphia in 1787, he outlined curricula for women's schools that deemphasized the "aristocratic, ornamental accomplishments" (dancing, etiquette, singing) and promoted "republican principles and knowledge" (ethics, history, math, science). Rush felt American women would achieve increased social and economic status in the Republic and accordingly should have the right to formal education.

Always a man with a wrong to right, Rush's energy never lagged even in his last years. His interests continued to be encyclopedic: he called for a temperance movement; urged development of the maple sugar industry to boycott the slave-produced sugar of the West Indies; crusaded for the abolition of loyalty oaths; and pressed for conservation of the nation's natural resources. He also reminisced with his revolutionary peers in an extensive correspondence that still sparkles with candor and sagacity. It was a Rush letter in 1811 that succeeded in reconciling his two friends, Thomas Jefferson and John Adams, politically estranged from each other since 1801. The result of Rush's intercession was the voluminous Adams-Jefferson correspondence that ranks as one of the most profound intellectual documents in American cultural history. When Rush died in 1813, many eulogized him, but none more appropriately than Jefferson writing to Adams: "Another of our friends of seventy-six is gone, my dear Sir, another of the co-signers of the Independence of our country. And better man than Rush could not have left us, more benevolent, more learned, of finer genius, or more honest."

Isaac Backus

MARTIN E. MARTY

Two hundred years after the birth of the United States, most Americans still have to face issues of church and state. Some Protestants are opposed to the idea that Catholic parochial school children should ride publicly supported buses. Little Amish school children are rounded up by law-enforcement officers because they go to their own "inadequate" schools. A child of Jehovah's Witness members needs a blood transfusion—and the state steps in to provide it, because the parents are opposed to such a

41

transfusion. Jews become nervous when public ceremonies sound too Christian. The majority of the people oppose two U. S. Supreme Court decisions of the sixties because these "took God out of the public schools."

Such debates have a long history. In a sense they never can be finally concluded. There are no permanent winners. Most people have commitments to both the civil and religious realms of life, and their interests often overlap and clash. The rights of the nonreligious have to be protected. Most of all, the United States is a "pluralistic" society, believing that any number of religions can coexist and that citizens should neither be praised nor blamed for holding or not holding to a particular doctrine or faith. Life in such a society can never be neat.

If good things have happened in America to enable people of different points of view to form a nation and to get along, they did not come about automatically. They had to be fought for. The United States has a gallery of heroes who have made contributions to the ways we have of relating church and state. Thomas Jefferson and James Madison are probably best known on the public side. Within the churches, names like William Penn and Roger Williams are familiar enough. Not only Catholics remember Cecilius Calvert, Lord Baltimore, who helped bring religious freedom to Maryland.

That gallery would not be complete without the name and face of Isaac Backus. I have no doubt that well over nine out of ten readers have never heard that name until this minute—including the Baptists (America's largest Protestant group) who stand in his tradition. Not everyone who contributes to the life we live is clearly remembered by name. And Backus was not a lonely, isolated figure; he was a leader among many who shared in the struggle for freedom. He was among the most consistent and doughtiest, however, and we will be well served by the bicentennial years if they help us become familiar with people who shared his vision and courage.

A *Who's Who* of early U.S. times would be able to locate Backus very simply. He was born in Norwich, Connecticut, 1724, and died in Middleboro, Massachusetts in 1806. He wrote a gigantic *History of New England, with Particular Reference to the Denomination of Christians Called Baptists.* This book was recently reprinted and is regularly used by people who write on the subject of church and state in America. He grew up in Congregationalism, but separated from it and became a Baptist. In 1756 he

42

organized the Baptist church at Middleboro and remained its minister. But a man of Backus's enthusiasms and involvements could not "stay put," and he was always on the move, talking at other churches and fighting for their rights. He is also remembered as a founder of Brown University in the 1760s.

Such bare biography does not catch much of the drama of Backus's life and contribution. In order to set the stage, we must picture the church situation in New England when he was a young man. No doubt most Americans to this day have a mental picture that their foreparents came to New England in order to provide religious freedom. They did—for themselves. They were very happy to have those who disagreed with them worship God as they saw fit: elsewhere. Dissenters from their Puritan and Congregational pattern were thus free to worship God in "Rogue's Island," better known as Rhode Island, where Baptists and others who did not fit in were at home from the first.

The Congregationalists, in short, set up a religious Establishment. Today we talk about "the Establishment" in informal terms. Whoever unofficially holds power can be part of it. Not so in colonial Connecticut and Massachusetts. There the Congregationalists held a privileged position. They received financial support from the taxpayers. For most of the seventeenth and early eighteenth century they controlled civic life. You had to be a converted member of the church in order to hold office or even to vote. Preachers at all public occasions would belong to the official church.

By the time of Backus, some of the more oppressive features of this system had been softened. It was convenient for the Establishment not to make waves, to provoke opposition. So its leaders could often wink a bit and allow more room for dissent. But that did not satisfy Isaac Backus. His principles simply would not allow for any official state-supported religion. We take such an approach so for granted today that it is hard to picture struggles over the issue.

Now comes the surprise: ordinarily those who are remembered for helping bring about the disestablishment of the churches and the separation of civil and religious realms ("church and state") are pictured as resenting privilege. They did not want to have to pay taxes for a religion they did not share. True enough. But Backus—like Roger Williams before him—had another, different, and to him bigger issue in mind. He was less worried about religion interfering in the state than he was about the state interfering with religion.

Today it may be hard to picture people taking religion and its purity that seriously. Not that there are not enough serious and sincere believers. But they have long been given the luxury of seeing their churches and synagogues uninterfered with. Most of them also let the state set more of the terms for their faith than they know. They usually have a national flag in their sanctuaries, not realizing that it can be made into an idol. They rarely speak up against any national policies that may threaten their faith. Nation and church are blended in their minds. In Backus's mind they were not; nor were they to be. They must be kept distinct. He might be (and was) a patriot of prominence. But that did not mean that either the states of Connecticut or Massachusetts or the United States dared interfere in any way with the purity of the church.

In order to be this consistent and concerned, Backus had to "get religion" with a rather heavy dose. In 1741 he was converted in what is still remembered as The Great Awakening, a time of religious revival and recovery. Today we think of Great Awakening preaching as emotional; it was, but such emotion was necessary to stir a quiet people. Backus was much stirred. But he was not content, as many converts at revivals have been, to stay at home and nurture his thoughts about himself and God. By 1749 he was in jail for refusing to pay a church tax. And he quickened others to similar activity. In 1770 he logged 2,058 saddle-sore miles; in 1789 he recorded 3,163 such miles.

Backus enters the history books in 1774, when he traveled to the Continental Congress and made his pitch for religious freedom to Boston's delegates and a few others. One exchange in Backus's meeting with these leaders shows how far apart from or ahead of them he was. John Adams and Samuel Adams did admit that "there is indeed an ecclesiastical establishment in our province; but a very slender one, hardly to be called an establishment." That was not good enough for a pure-church defender. The principle was what mattered. When Backus left, John Adams told him, "We might as soon expect a change in the solar system as to expect that [the citizens] would give up their establishment." The change in the solar system did not occur; it took almost fifty years for Massachusetts to make up its mind decisively.

In effect, Backus and his fellow Baptists were fighting a war within the Revolutionary War. While supporting the colonies' cause, they also were willing to embarrass the revolutionaries if they felt that these were not consistent about freedoms. How could one fight for freedom from British oppression and continue to oppress fellow colonists whose faith differed from the established version? After Backus had met with the group that included the four Boston delegates, rumors reached Massachusetts that he was trying to prevent the unification of the colonies. Some historians in our own time still consider his act ill-advised, given the fragile character of American union at the time. Whether Backus had much impact then or not is not known. It is difficult to picture him being silenced for strategic reasons, to act against principle just because of a war.

When the Federal Constitution was completed at Philadelphia in 1787, Backus was elected a delegate to the Massachusetts convention that had to decide about ratifying it. "As religious liberty is concerned in the affair, and many were earnest for my going, I consented." While he had some disagreements with the Constitution, he was for it chiefly because it excluded religious tests for public office. The Constitution won in Massachusetts, 187–168. Full religious freedom did not come in his state, however, until 1833—twenty-seven years after his death. Backus never was allowed to lapse back into genteel retirement from the fray.

While Thomas Jefferson and his colleagues looked ahead to a happier day with America as a new center of learning and progress, Backus foresaw that America would represent a new enlargement of God's kingdom. The Warren Association, of which he was a part, in 1784 wrote, "Nor is it at all improbable that America is reserved in the mind of Jehovah to be the grand theatre on which the divine Redeemer will accomplish glorious things. . . . If we observe the signs of the times, we shall find reason to think he is on his way." Little wonder that such Baptists would encourage their fellow-believers to be positive participants in the state and in society. Here they went beyond their predecessor Roger Williams, who was so interested in a pure church that he feared that believers would be tainted if they had much contact with the world.

Backus was not a highly educated man nor an original thinker. Today the scholars sort out which ideas he got from the age's greatest theologian, Jonathan Edwards, or from a philosopher who had much influence on colonial leaders, John Locke. He was informed by Locke and particularly his *The Letter on Toleration.* But we should not picture him as a quiet scholar whiling away the hours in Lockean libraries. He was a man of action who was not afraid of causes that were not popular. Out of his own experience he was able to propose plans and patterns that have helped shape the later American experience. That he reached for Locke and other more profound thinkers in order to bolster his points was a natural and wise thing to do. He wanted to broaden his base as much as possible. The issue of religious freedom needed all the friends it could get. Backus should be remembered as a tireless "man on the road" rustling up support.

People who 200 years later have much less loyalty to the church than did he, or who have no feeling at all for his Baptist faith, live and breathe more freely as a result of his religious experience—and the conscience formed by it.

Henry David Thoreau

PATRICIA McNEAL

Enter any bookstore in the United States and you will find a book written by Henry David Thoreau. Though he was unheralded in his own lifetime, his writings capture the attention of today's reading public. His popularity is rooted in his lifelong crusade both in word and deed to uphold the supreme dignity of the individual. What he did for America was to open the democratic vista—to proclaim to the world that a million men are of no importance compared with one man.

In 1776 Americans were summoned to preserve the blessings of liberty; sixty years later an obscure New Englander reminded his contemporaries that the strength of the nation depended on the freedom and truth found in each individual American. Today Americans are seeking to recapture this spirit of freedom and truth. Upset with a lack of integrity in the public sector and the invasion of individual freedom, many people are contending, like Thoreau, that the revolution of 1776 will not endure unless each person undergoes his or her own revolution by affirming in word and deed the truth and freedom of one's individual person.

The one-man revolution in which all may participate has been exemplified in our history by Henry David Thoreau. He was born the third child of John and Cynthia Thoreau on July 12, 1817, in Concord, Massachusetts. He attended Concord Academy; at considerable financial sacrifice to his family, Thoreau entered Harvard College in the fall of 1833. Despite two long periods of absence (one because of illness and the other to earn money for his tuition) he did well in his classses—so well in fact, that he was asked to read an honors paper at his commencement exercises in 1837. Characteristically, he went against the trend of his times and asked his fellow graduates to reverse the biblical maxim by working one day a week and resting six.

When Thoreau graduated from Harvard, "the air was full of reform": the main social issues were slavery, temperance, women's rights, and prison reform. The philosophy of transcendentalism had reached its heyday and it provided the main impetus for many reform movements. Transcendentalism was rooted in the principle of the supreme dignity of the individual. As a school of thought it attempted to reorient the possibilities of life, to give to the individual new powers and a new stage for actions; it desired to make all things new.

It was transcendentalism that shaped and sanctioned Thoreau's youthful aspirations. This is not surprising since the small village of Concord with its population of only 2,000 was the center of transcendentalism. The young Harvard graduate was admitted into the circle of lofty thinkers and well-known writers (such as Nathaniel Hawthorne, Margaret Fuller, and Bronson Alcott) because of his friendship with Ralph Waldo Emerson, the chief sage of the transcendentalists. This group made Concord the Athens of New England.

To the people of Concord, however, Thoreau was a freak; even his intellectual confreres, except Emerson, were not certain whether he was a genius or a fake. Such judgments of Thoreau are readily understandable since he was never in step with the trend of his times. Even in appearance Thoreau was different. He was short, longarmed, "as ugly as sin, longnosed, queer-mouthed, and with uncouth and somewhat rustic, although courteous manners." Sometimes he was even mistaken for a peddler or a tramp. Such incidents flattered him and he congratulated himself upon "enjoying the unusual advantage of being the humblest, cheapest, least dignified man in the village."

By choice Thoreau refused to say what he did for a living. He did not want to be labeled by the limitation of a particular job or task. During his lifetime, he was an occasional teacher, surveyor, seldom wanted lecturer, pencil maker, nature lover, and writer. Though he is remembered today as a writer, he made *living*—not writing—his goal. It was his search of learning *how* to live that brought him lasting fame. He refused to try to succeed in an approved way. As he put it, "The life which men prize and regard as successful is but one kind. Why should we exaggerate any one kind at the expense of the others?" Thus, he refused to bend to the pressures of society by defining his life in terms of a job. Basically, he was revolting against society and its institutions which he believed had been deformed by the crudities of an expanding capitalism. Instead, Thoreau battled for self-determination by developing himself as fully as possible. Only later did he write about his experiences.

In the late fall of 1844, Thoreau had the opportunity to try living the simple life. Emerson had purchased much of the land around the shore of Walden Pond, a beautiful glacial lake less than two miles from Concord village, to preserve it from a woodchopper's axe. In return for clearing some of the scrub land at the pond and reforesting it with pines, Emerson allowed Thoreau to build a cabin on the land and live there rent free.

Thoreau went to Walden because he realized that living such a simple life would give him a new experience and the economic freedom necessary for writing. Ever since the death of his brother John in 1842, he had wished to write an account of their vacation together on the Concord and Merrimack Rivers in 1839; at Walden Pond he wrote that book. He also finished the first draft of what would become one of the great classics in American literature, *Walden.*

"Two years, two months, and two days" after going to live at Walden Pond, he abandoned his retreat. "I left the woods for as good a reason as I went there," he said. "Perhaps it seemed that I had several more lives to live, and could not spare any more time for that one."

In 1848 Thoreau negotiated a contract with James Munroe & Co. for the publication of *A Week on the Concord and Merrimack Rivers*— guaranteeing to underwrite the cost of the book, if it did not sell. It was issued in May of 1849 and the sales of the book could hardly be termed "rousing." Munroe demanded payment of the cost of publication and returned to Thoreau 706 copies out of an edition of 1,000. To conceal his disappointment and to attempt to maintain his humor, Thoreau commented that he now had "a library of nearly nine hundred volumes, over seven hundred of which I wrote myself." The total project cost Thoreau $290; a century later, copies of the first edition of this work bring hundreds of dollars apiece.

This was not the case with *Walden,* the only other book of Thoreau's published during his lifetime. He revised the original draft eight times before it was finally published in 1854. The nearly 3,000 copies sold netted Thoreau a profit commensurate with his loss on *A Week.* Since 1854 *Walden* has never been out of print and has appeared in over 150 different editions. It has been translated into sixteen foreign languages.

In *Walden,* Thoreau provides a searching account for the desire to discover a new kind of life. Criticizing contemporary life, he proclaims that Americans "have the Saint Vitus dance," diverting their energies to material expansion. He is also concerned with the life of quiet desperation which he believes most Americans lead and the economic fallacy which is responsible for the situation in which they find themselves. As a cure for mankind, Thoreau prescribes the following: a total renunciation of the traditional, the conventional, the socially acceptable, and the total immersion in nature. He emphasizes the importance of man's correspondence with nature, and argues for the almost limitless possibilities of individual inspiration and achievement. Through the simple life of immersion in nature, man will perceive the "higher law" through transcendental insight and become a man of freedom and truth.

Besides Thoreau's love of nature and the simple life, the other main reason for his success stems from his writings on political theory—the core of which is his concept of individual action.

Early one July evening in 1846, on his way to Concord from his Walden cabin to get a shoe that was being repaired, Thoreau was arrested. The charge was nonpayment of his poll tax, not paid since 1842 as a protest against slavery. In 1846 when Thoreau went to jail, the war in Mexico was beginning, a war which Thoreau believed was undertaken by the United States on behalf of slaveholders who wished to extend their slave territory. In response to this situation, Thoreau asked, "How does it become a man to behave toward this American government today?"

It was apparently Thoreau's intention to bring about a test case of the poll-tax law, but his Aunt Maria intervened and paid the tax and ruined his opportunity. Instead, he turned to writing an essay, "Civil Disobedience," to get his idea across. Thoreau's aim in the essay was to move men away from adherence to insidious relativism and persuade them to return again to the superior standard of absolute truth. When moral and governmental law come into conflict, Thoreau argued that "it is not desirable to cultivate a respect for the law, so much as for the right." And the most effective way to do this according to Thoreau was by practicing "civil disobedience"; in his case this meant refusing to pay taxes and going to jail. According to Thoreau, by practicing civil disobedience, the individual would obstruct the governmental process and win sympathy through martyrdom. The individual's willingness to suffer for what is right would arouse the citizenry to an awareness of the wrong and a willingness to right it.

Thoreau's idea of civil disobedience spread. His essay served as a textbook for Gandhi in India and even more recently for Martin Luther King, Jr. in his civil rights campaign in America. The essay, "Civil Disobedience," has been widely printed and is perhaps more frequently read than *Walden.* But "Civil Disobedience" is less a declaration of any intention to become a social reformer than a reaffirmation of Thoreau's defiant individualism. Thoreau was not interested in politics; he was concerned about the individual. Reform the individual and society would not need reformation.

It is not surprising that Thoreau never gained popular acclaim during his lifetime. He was out of step with his times; indeed, ahead of his time. Only after his death on May 6, 1862, when tuberculosis took his life at the early age of forty-four, did he begin to receive recognition as a writer. With each succeeding generation his fame has increased. Mainly, because so much of what he had written about the efforts of the individual to live his own life in truth and freedom have attained increasing validity in face of America's unbridled technological and material expansion.

Today, at a time when the individual is seemingly becoming less and less important, the spirit of Thoreau and his one-man revolution takes on an added significance. His life and his writings are a challenge to every person to pursue the path of individual freedom and wage his or her own revolution. This challenge became most explicit and indeed most popularized in his memorable verse from *Walden:*

> If a man does not keep pace
> with his companions, perhaps it is
> because he hears a different drummer.
> Let him step to the music which he hears,
> however measured or far away.

Harriet Tubman

BENJAMIN QUARLES

"I grew up like a neglected weed—ignorant of liberty, having no experience of it." The speaker, a short, spare, black-skinned woman, her heavy-lidded eyes deep-set and shing, was being interviewed by journalist Benjamin Drew at her home in St. Catherines, Ontario, in the summer of 1855. "Now, I've been free," she added, "I know what a dreadful condition slavery is."

The speaker, thirty-five-year-old Harriet Ross Tubman, had not yet achieved the fame that four years later would prompt the reformer and

57

author, Thomas Wentworth Higginson, to dub her "the greatest heroine of the age." But from the time of her escape from slavery in 1849, the spell of freedom had been upon her, impelling her to seek it for others. The phrase, "the blessings of liberty," which the Founding Fathers had put in the Constitution, took on a special meaning to one who had been a slave for nearly thirty years.

Harriet had few pleasant memories of her years in bondage in Dorchester County, not far from the town of Cambridge on Maryland's Eastern Shore. She was one of eleven children of Harriet Greene and Benjamin Ross, both slaves; her childhood experiences were dominated by hard work and mistreatment. Put to work when she was almost five, she served in turn as maid, child's nurse and, by the time she was twelve, as a field hand.

While still in her teens, she was struck on the head by a two-pound weight hurled at another slave whom she attempted to shield from the wrath of an overseer. From this nearly fatal blow she never fully recovered; she was prone to seizures of deep, sudden sleep from time to time for the rest of her long life. She did regain her strength, however, her capacity for manual labor rivaling that of a man by the time she was twenty.

Harriet Ross's hard life in slavery was lessened a little by her marriage in 1844. Her husband, John Tubman, a free black, lacked his wife's will power and sense of mission. He scoffed at her fears and forebodings. He did not fully reciprocate her deep affection for him; he did not join her when she made the dash for freedom.

One of Harriet Tubman's forebodings, the dread of being sold to the Deep South, took on a new intensity in 1849 upon the death of her master and the rumor that his estate would be broken up and his property dispersed. Deciding to delay no longer, Harriet made the break for freedom. Traveling by night, she finally arrived in free-soil Pennsylvania. She felt like she was in heaven. "There was such a glory over everything," she said. "The sun came like gold through the trees, and over the fields."

This mood of exultation was quickly followed by one of almost religious dedication. Tubman resolved on the spot that inasmuch as she was now free, she would strive to bring freedom to others. She would become a conductor on the underground railroad—that organized effort to assist slaves in running away from their masters.

Her schemes required money, so Tubman came to Philadelphia and took work in a hotel, the first in a series of part-time jobs. After a year of penny-pinching frugality, she had saved enough to launch her first expedition—the rescue of her sister, Mary Ann Bowley, and her two children. Harriet had financed Mary Ann's flight from Cambridge to Baltimore, where the two sisters met, and the point at which the more experienced Harriet took charge.

To give a connected recital of Harriet Tubman's subsequent journeys into slave locales is not possible. Insofar as she could, she operated in secrecy. Had she been able to read and write, she would hardly have kept any written records. In her some ten years of underground railroad operations, she made at least 15 rescue trips and and personally escorted at least 200 runaways. To these minimum numbers, however, must be added a factor not easy to measure but important nonetheless. Tubman was an inspiration to thousands whom she would never meet, giving new hope to many slaves and new zeal to many abolitionist crusaders. Whether in the flesh or as a symbol, she made slave property less secure.

If we cannot give a trip-by-trip account of Harriet's rescue journeys, we can better assess the overall reasons for their success. These were twofold: her stamina and personality, and her methods of operation.

Wearing a bandana or, occasionally, a floppy sunbonnet, Tubman was not impressive in appearance. "A more ordinary specimen of humanity could hardly be found among the most unfortunate-looking farmhands of the South," wrote William Still. But she had great powers of endurance, seldom showing signs of fatigue.

She was courageous, undeterred by the knowledge that there was a price upon her head. Her bravery was matched, moreover, by her coolness in a tight spot. If the fugitives she led lacked her fearlessness, they were silenced by her blunt, no-nonsense manner while on the journey.

Her strong character came from her total and absolute faith in God. She felt that Divine Providence had willed her freedom and that a guardian angel accompanied her, particularly on her missions of deliverance. When the slaves gave her the name Moses, she did not demur. Spirituals and gospel exhortations came readily to her lips.

Tubman's trust in God did not lull her into neglecting the exercise of great care in planning her rescue missions. Among underground railroad conductors she was without peer in anticipating the needs of her fugitive flock, whether food or clothes, disguises or forged passes, wagons or train tickets.

To obtain funds for her operations, including payment to those who would give refuge to slaves, she took whatever jobs that came her way. As her fame spread, however, she supplemented her own earnings by taking up collections at abolitionist gatherings.

Mrs. Tubman's careful planning included her full cooperation with like-minded spirits. She worked hand in hand with two of the country's most dedicated station masters on the underground railroad, Thomas Garrett in Wilmington and William Still in Philadelphia. Garrett, a white Quaker, soft-spoken but powerfully built, was not one to be intimidated by slave-catchers. The energetic and resourceful William Still, whose parents had been slaves, was second only to Harriet among the blacks who worked in the underground railroad. Both Garrett and Still assisted Harriet by providing shelter for the fugitive groups she conducted and by making arrangements for their transportation further north.

With her plans made and her contacts alerted, Harriet was ready to lead her charges. As a rule she began her return trips on a Saturday night. This meant that there was little likelihood that the hue and cry over the missing slaves could be raised until Monday, thus giving the escaping party a day's grace. Harriet made it a point to hire a resident black to tear down all notices that had been posted concerning the runaways. Once on the road she seemed to have a sixth sense in foraging for food and in selecting hiding places in the woods. She carried drugs for fretful babies whose crying might jeopardize the escaping party. She also carried a rifle, not only for protection but also to keep in line anyone who became faint of heart and wished to turn back.

Although she could boast that she never lost a passenger on the underground railroad, one of her trips was less than a complete success. In the fall of 1851 she made a journey to the locale of her early years, bent on persuading John Tubman to leave Dorchester County and go northward with her. She found that her erstwhile husband had taken another wife, however, whom he was not disposed to leave. But if John would not join her, others would; hence she rounded up a party of fugitives to accompany her on the return trip.

60

If the failure to reclaim her former husband was Mrs. Tubman's most disappointing trip, the rescue of her own parents, in June 1857, was undoubtedly the most satisfying. Harriet's father, faced with punishment for assisting a runaway, finally yielded to Harriet's urgings to flee to freedom. Because her parents were unable to walk long distances, Harriet rigged up a makeshift wagon, with herself as its driver. "With such an experienced guide as Harriet, they passed safely on," wrote Thomas Garrett, who met them in Wilmington.

Harriet settled her parents in Auburn, New York, on land she had purchased from an admirer, Senator William H. Seward. She had moved to Auburn two years before her last rescue mission, when she brought seven slaves from southern Maryland on December 30, 1860. Until 1859 her home base had been St. Catherines, Ontario, where most of the 800 blacks were, like Harriet, runaway slaves.

It was at St. Catherines, in early April 1858, that Mrs. Tubman first met John Brown, who had made the trip expressly to enlist her services. Brown felt that Harriet would be invaluable, both in enlisting volunteers for his army of liberation and as a conductor-guide to the slaves he planned to set free. Brown's meeting with Harriet was all he could have wished, leading him to keep in touch with her. But in October 1859, when Brown and his band made the assault on Harpers Ferry, Harriet was absent, having fallen sick late that summer.

The outbreak of the Civil War, fanned in part by the John Brown raid, was a development Harriet Tubman had predicted. Viewing the war as the climax of the crusade against slavery, she was determined to become a participant. Early in 1862 she went to the South Carolina seacoast region, with Beaufort as her headquarters. Here for three years she assisted the newly freed slaves, working primarily as a nurse and cook. Her hospital employment was punctuated by work with the Union army as a spy and a scout.

Regardless of their nature, her war-related services found a ready welcome. Wherever she went she hardly needed the letters of recommendation she carried, whether from civilian officials such as Governor John A. Andrew of Massachusetts or military authorities such as Generals Rufus Saxton and David Hunter.

The end of the war in 1865 did not mean the end of Harriet's career of service to others. During the remaining half century she was to live, she was always active on behalf of the less fortunate, engaging in such activities as raising money for schools for former slaves, collecting clothes for destitute children, or establishing a home for the aged poor. She assumed the complete care and support of her parents.

Her management of fiscal affairs, although scrupulously honest, was somewhat impulsive. Her way of administering a fund, according to a fellow Auburnite who knew her well, was "to give away all the money she had upon her at the moment and trust to the good Lord to fill the void."

In doing charitable work, however, she was not discouraged by a chronic lack of funds and the absence of a personal income until she was over seventy-five. From her own wartime services she had received no benefits despite the support of her petitions by prominent citizens. In 1890, following the death of Nelson Davis, a Union soldier she had married in March 1869, she was awarded a pension of eight dollars a month, subsequently increased to twenty dollars a month.

Harriet Tubman died on March 10, 1913, appropriately enough in the home for the elderly that bore her name as its founder, and that she had willed to the African Methodist Zion Church. Perhaps, too, it was not inappropriate that the Auburn Post of the Grand Army of the Republic took part in the funeral exercises. Later in the spring a memorial service was held by the city of Auburn, whose mayor asked that on that day every home fly the Stars and Stripes, thus demonstrating that "we are not forgetful of those who suffered for the cause of freedom and were willing to die that we might have one country and one flag."

A person worthy of such a tribute is worthy of another look in these bicentennial times. More than a tale of adventure, more even than a personal triumph over color and sex, Harriet Tubman's life symbolized the quest for human dignity. Her career was a quest for the truths which the Declaration of Independence proclaimed were self-evident, and to which the Constitution and the Bill of Rights bore early witness. She personified the greatest American freedom movement of the nineteenth century—the crusade against slavery.

During World War II a liberty ship was christened, "Harriet Tubman," prompting President Franklin D. Roosevelt to praise the U. S.

Maritime Commission for having chosen so appropriate a name. In a time of war, such as then, or in a time of national commemoration, such as now, a figure like Harriet Tubman demands our reflection. She embodied the great affirmations that marked the birth of the Republic.

Thomas Edison

MATTHEW JOSEPHSON

Among those we like to honor as the "builders" of America, Thomas A. Edison surely ranks high. One of the most prolific inventors the world has ever known, awarded 1,093 patents during his lifetime, Edison was a leader in the march of mankind—for better or worse—toward the Age of Technology. He stemmed from the breed of old-fashioned Yankee inventors who, by cut-and-try methods, contrived an impressive quantity of new mechanical devices. Even though he was without formal scientific education, Edison went on to introduce momentous changes in the very process of invention, mainly by systematic experimentation and extensive research in the light of such modern science as he knew. Whole new industries sprang from the hands of this inventive genius and old industries were given a swifter tempo. He grew rich and world famous, and enriched others by creating so much new wealth, yet he worked on all his life like a titan. For half a century the public hero-worshipped the former trainboy, for he embodied the fulfillment of the American dream of rags-to-riches through sharp wits and hard work.

Thomas Alva Edison was born in Milan, Ohio, on February 11, 1847, the youngest of four children of Samuel Ogden and Nancy Elliott. When he was seven, his father, a small merchant in building materials, came on hard times, and the family moved to Port Huron, Michigan. There in a one-room schoolhouse, the boy received his only formal schooling during three months, after which the schoolmaster ejected him as "retarded." His mother, who had formerly taught school, then undertook to tutor him at home for the next three years. "She instilled in me the love and purpose of learning," Edison said in recollection.

He was a hyperactive boy, endlessly curious, and much given to pranks, so that his father birched him regularly. Middle-ear deafness, resulting from scarlatina, added to his difficulties and contributed to his forming shy and solitary habits. One day when he was about ten his mother brought him an elementary science book, which strongly aroused the boy's interest. In the cellar of his home he set up a small chemical laboratory and tested out every experiment in the book. After a while he was able to make his own wetcell batteries, producing electric current, and operating a homemade telegraph set. As Thomas seemed to live only for his crude telegraphs and little steam engines, his father said of him that "he never had a boyhood or played out of doors like other boys."

The father continued to be a poor provider, so when Thomas was twelve he went to work on the new railroad between Port Huron and Detroit as a train newsboy. Somehow he managed to install his boy's laboratory in a baggage car; amid the uproar of the train (which he heard not), and during layovers in the Detroit yard, he continued his "experiments" and extended his reading of popular scientific books and journals. Those long days away from home, selling newspapers and candy, but mostly learning by himself about things that interested him, he described later as the happiest time of

66

his life. When he was sixteen he had trained himself as a telegrapher, for he could hear without interference the high click of his instrument; and after 1863 he roamed the country as a "tramp telegrapher," working some of the time in the South, behind the battlefronts of the Civil War, but usually in the Midwest. For five years he was one of the bohemian breed of telegraphers that flourished in the 1860s. Their roving style of life suited him; he chose to work the night shift, which allowed him to spend the daylight hours in cheap furnished rooms, almost without sleep, in interminable experiments in manipulating electrical currents. His object in life was to increase the speed and capacity of the telegraph; nearly all that he earned went for chemicals and electrical equipment.

At twenty-one, Edison was a lonely eccentric, personable, but ill-kempt and rustic-looking. Yet he won the notice of his coworkers by his remarkable powers of observation and his fine thumb for "curing" troubled telegraph sets. It was around that time, while working in Boston, that he bought a secondhand copy of Michael Faraday's journals, *Experimental Researches in Electricity*, which he read in a day and a night. This marked a turning point in his life. The great English scientist had been self-taught; Edison too would extend his self-education by performing all the experiments Faraday had set forth so clearly. Henceforth his investigations were more painstaking and were recorded in laboratory notebooks; he worked over his schemes in a sort of frenzy. Soon, with a little borrowed money, he launched himself as a free-lance inventor.

One day in the autumn of 1868 he appeared in Washington before a committee of Congress with his first patented invention, an electric vote-recording machine, which he held would save time and trouble. When the statesmen ruled that this was just what they did *not* want, Edison realized that his inventions had to be *practical*—a lesson he always remembered. A few months later the penniless inventor was sleeping in a basement in Wall Street, New York, next to a ponderous telegraphic machine that indicated current prices on the Gold Exchange upstairs. At a moment of crisis he was called upon to repair the balky instrument, which he did so well that he was given a job as its inspector. Its owners, the Western Union, also commissioned him to improve upon the first crude version of a telegraphic stock ticker. Edison then developed his own original model, the Edison Universal Stock Printer; this, together with several other telegraphic inventions, brought him a sudden fortune of $40,000!

There followed an interlude of five years during which he performed both as an inventor and a rising capitalist, running two factories in Newark, New Jersey, turning out stock tickers and telegraph instruments. He prospered, was married, and had his first two children, but he was seldom seen at home, as he continued to be a "fiend for work," in the view of his chief clients, the Western Union Company. That organization, then ruled by the Vanderbilts and J. P. Morgan, had a powerful rival in the railroad baron Jay Gould; Edison, like a scientific soldier of fortune, sometimes tried working for Gould, who ended, as often happened, by swindling the inventor.

The cares of commercial life vexed and wearied him. He feared, as he said, that he might become a "mere bloated Eastern manufacturer." His ruling passion was for truly inventive work; indeed he always kept a little office in one of his shops where he experimented with new products that excited him, such as a quadruplex (high speed) telegraph, and even a crude electric light that would not stay lit.

In the spring of 1876, moved by a sudden whim, he disposed of his factories and moved out to the hamlet of Menlo Park, New Jersey, some twenty-five miles from New York. There he constructed a two-story wooden frame building that looked like a rural meeting house, which he equipped as a full-fledged research laboratory. An impressive quantity of scientific instruments and newfangled machines were installed in it, including a Brown steam engine, a forge, induction coils, galvanometers, electrometers, and a store of chemicals and metals; he also set up an extensive library of scientific journals and technical books. Some twenty skilled machinists and clockmakers who had served under him at Newark were persuaded to come and work at Menlo Park, where they were to form a team of specialists carrying out systematic investigations under his command. His establishment, he announced, would be "an all-purpose research laboratory" and "invention factory." Indeed, he boasted at the start to a scientific friend that he would turn out a "minor invention" every ten days and some "big thing" every six months.

Such was the world's first industrial research laboratory, where Edison planned to give himself entirely to research and development, and where he knew his finest hours. In one of his first (ill-spelled) letters from Menlo Park, he declared himself wonderfully happy again and invited a friend to come out to his "brand new laboratory... planet Earth,

Middlesex County, on the Pennsylvania Railroad... on a high hill, the prettiest spot in New Jersey. Will show you around, go strawberrying."

There were then only a few laboratories in the country as well equipped as Edison's; they were located at the leading universities, but were devoted to the advancement of pure scientific knowledge. Edison desired above all to make his investigations *practical,* and boasted that he would "make inventions to order." As the German historian Werner Sombart wrote, Edison "made a *business* of invention," formerly the occupation of poor, uninformed, and traditionally luckless mechanics working at a bench in a factory or in some attic. Edison, for his part, believed that he was organizing things in a democratic spirit to create useful devices that would fill real needs and lighten human drudgery.

By a historic coincidence Edison's industrial research laboratory was launched in the centennial year of this Republic; from Menlo Park there flowed a stream of inventions of high originality which soon effected tremendous changes in our whole way of life, while later on giant industrial research laboratories, in imitation of Edison's little institution, arose everywhere to speed change further.

Bell's telephone was the sensation of the Philadelphia Exposition of 1876. Its poor audibility, however, was fully corrected a year later by Edison's invention of the (separate) carbon transmitter. The highly imaginative Edison had the gift of serendipity; turning off course for some unexpected phenomenon he had perceived, he quickly produced the phonograph, his most original invention, based on fresh observations of sound dynamics. It was an example of the bold simplicity of many of his best devices, which is the mark of great inventors. Not only was it loved by the multitudes, but great scientists like Helmholtz admired it, and with it Edison achieved world fame.

Having seen the glaring new arc-lights of 500 candlepower at Philadelphia in 1876, he publicly boasted that he would invent a mild, safe, and economical electric light, whose current would be subdivided and distributed by his own system so that it would replace the gaslight used by millions. A syndicate of financiers, including J. P. Morgan and the Vanderbilts, soon came forward to advance $50,000 for research and development of his incandescent light, which had been the despair of the world's inventors for fifty years. There followed the famous dragnet search for a usable

69

filament which the Menlo Park team pursued night and day for fourteen months. On October 21, 1879, a pilot station of thirty carbon filament lamps in parallel circuit, supplied with current by Edison's own constant-voltage dynamo, lit up the night at Menlo Park before a great crowd of visitors. The affair involved also scores of complementary inventions making a novel system of control and distribution of current. Three years later the first central power and light station opened for business in downtown New York; other cities of the world followed suit.

In the 1880s Edison left Menlo Park, having become involved in the growing industries that sprang up from his inventions, Edison Electric Light and Edison General Electric. After the death of his first wife he married Mina Miller, a younger woman of excellent family. A multimillionaire, the eccentric tobacco-chewing inventor lived in a mansion at suburban West Orange, New Jersey. Nearby he built a much larger research laboratory and surrounded it with big factories turning out the new products he continued to invent, including his improved phonograph, a nickel-iron storage battery, a motion picture projector. The achievements of his later years, however, were not as spectacular as those of his young manhood at Menlo Park. His want of theoretical science—of which he boasted in public, as if making it a virtue—also told against him in later years, as in the case of his stubborn opposition to high-voltage alternating currents—in favor of his limited direct current system—which were successfully introduced by rivals, such as Westinghouse, with the help of a new generation of scientists.

One accidental discovery of no little importance, which he failed to understand, was of an unwonted flow of current between two electrodes in a vacuum bulb. This he patented in 1883, and it became known to history as the "Edison effect." Long years afterward J. J. Thomson, while studying such phenomena, discovered the electron; and after that came De Forest's vacuum tube. Thus Edison served as the careless progenitor of radio and electronics!

Sometimes he lost whole fortunes in projects such as his ore-milling venture, saying afterward: "Well, we had a hell of a good time losing it." Then he would recoup with something like the motion picture projector, and plunge again into new and hazardous ventures. Why? "To invent more!" he said.

70

The American people did not love the financial empire builders, the Morgans and Rockefellers, as they loved Edison, one of their great folk heroes. When he died in 1931 he was mourned by the nation as a "doer," "forever making things," a creative man in an age of acquisitors. For the great public he dramatized the life and labor of scientific invention as no other did. As one admirer wrote him: "You have made your success by hard work and brains and not by exploiting other men's work."

In his private character he was a benevolent tyrant to his family and his workers, whom he kept amused by his imagination and humor. In public, in his old age, he posed as a spirited autodidact and cracker-barrel philosopher, speaking for old-fashioned American individualism and political conservatism. He used to gibe at the "long-haired" scientists of the universities, and they assailed him as a mere "mechanic." His 3,400 notebooks show that he had a wide understanding of the principles of science as known in his time, and employed eminent mathematical physicists to aid him in his laboratory. A just view of Edison's role was Norbert Wiener's, who held that he was a transitional figure in the nineteenth century, arriving when crude mechanical inventors were to be replaced by specialized men pursuing systematic experiments and research on a large scale. After all it was Edison who established the first industrial research laboratory, in itself his greatest invention.

Helen Hunt Jackson

VINCENT P. DeSANTIS

"President after president has appointed commission after commission to inquire into and report upon Indian affairs, and to make suggestions as to the best methods of managing them," the roused Helen Hunt Jackson wrote in her powerful book *A Century of Dishonor* (1881), a classic statement of American injustice to the American Indian. She went on to say the federal Indian reports were "filled with eloquent statements of wrongs done to the Indians, [and] of perfidies on the part of the Government." And, she deplored the fact these accounts "are bound up with the

Government's Annual Reports, and that is the end of them. It would probably be no exaggeration to say that not one American citizen out of ten thousand ever sees them or knows that they exist," she continued, "and yet any one of them, circulated throughout the country . . . would initiate a revolution which would not subside until the Indians' wrongs were, so far as is now left possible, righted."

At the time Mrs. Jackson wrote these words, the United States was approaching the end of almost twenty-five years of continuous and brutal wars with the American Indians. And in some quarters there was a feeling something should be done to heal the deep wounds inflicted on the Indians by the nation.

An essential step in the conquest of the Last West after the Civil War was the solution of "the Indian question." Plainly and simply this was the fact that the Indian was in the white man's way as he pushed relentlessly westward over the Great Plains in search of lands to settle and resources to exploit. The Indians of the Great Plains and the Rocky Mountains actively opposed white settlement on their lands. The land had been theirs for centuries, and they were determined to fight, if necessary, to keep it. Mounted on swift horses and armed with bows and arrows they were more than a match for the white man until he perfected the repeater rifle.

Until the Civil War, the Plains Indians had been relatively peaceful. Then miners invaded the mountains, cattlemen moved into the grasslands, and white settlers followed the railroads across the prairies. Wanton destruction of the buffalo by intruding whites threatened the Indians' very existence, because they depended upon this animal for food, fuel, clothing, tools, and other essentials.

After the Civil War, General William Tecumseh Sherman was assigned the task of bringing peace to the Great Plains. His favorite word for accomplishing this was "extermination." He was determined the Indians were going to obey or be wiped out. In 1867, Congress enacted legislation providing for the removal of all Indians to reservations, thereby breaking the promises the nation had given to the Plains Indians in the 1820s and 1830s that they could keep their lands forever. Sherman expressed a prevalent white attitude at that time when he wrote, "We have . . . provided reservations for all, off the great roads. All who cling to their old hunting grounds are hostile and will remain so till killed off."

74

By relentless pursuit and with some indiscriminate slaughter of peaceful villages, Sherman's forces were able to bring the Indians to heel within a year. Chiefs of all the tribes signed treaties in the spring of 1868 accepting residence on reservations.

But then there was trouble. Many young Indians would not assent to the indignity of being placed on a reservation. While tribal chieftains signed the removal treaties many individual Indians refused to be bound by them. As hunters and nomads they were not willing to give up their ancient lands and freedom of movement to accept a confined and prosaic way of life on reservations. The Indians could not understand the white man's land hunger. To the Indians the earth and its creatures and resources belonged to all, the free gift of the Great Spirit. That one should build a fence around the land and say "This is mine" was repugnant to the Indians. Thus by the fall of 1868, within months after the signing of the reservation treaties, warfare between the United States Army and the Indians was in full swing on the Great Plains, and it lasted for ten years. Even after that time, scattered outbreaks continued for years. And it might have gone on beyond the 1880s had it not been for the immense buffalo herds, giving life and independence to the Plains Indians, being virtually wiped out. In about twenty years— from the early 1860s to 1883—the buffalo was practically exterminated from about 13 million of them to a mere 200.

The Indian Wars on the Plains were conducted in an intense and savage way on both sides. "When dealing with savage men, as with savage beasts, no question of national honor can arise," said General Francis A Walker, Commissioner of Indian Affairs, in 1871. A few years earlier General S.R. Curtis, United States Commander in the West, had told his subordinate officers, "I want no peace till the Indians suffer more." And the Indians did suffer. A white trader reported the Cheyenne "were scalped, their brains knocked out; the men used their knives, ripped open women, clubbed little children, knocked them in the head with their guns, beat their brains out, mutilated their bodies in every sense of the word." Such barbarity surely raises the question: Who were the savages, the Indians or the whites?

The Indian wars after 1865 cost the United States government millions of dollars and hundreds of lives, yet a solution to the problem seemed to be nowhere in sight. Frontiersmen in general believed the only good Indian was a dead one, and most soldiers in the West agreed. For the "great cause of civilization," said a government inspector in 1858, we "must exterminate Indians." And a newspaper in Yreka, a trading town in the California-Oregon border country declared in regard to Indians, "Let our motto be extermination, and death to all opposers."

At the bottom of these Indian wars was the white man's all consuming greed for property. Over and over again mining, railroad, and land-speculation interests were able to pressure the federal government to persuade or to force the Indians to accept altered treaties and changed reservations. And each time this happened a solemn promise of the United States was broken and Indian distrust of anything American or white increased. General George Crook, one of the most famous western Indian fighters, observed what was happening in this way: "Greed and avarice on the part of whites—in other words the almighty dollar, is at the bottom of nine-tenths of all our Indian troubles."

In the Americans's conquest of the West, their treatment of the Indians was a national disgrace. It is one of the most shameful blots on our history and one still strongly affecting our national conscience. They cheated the Indians at every turn. They made solemn agreements they did not keep. They shot down defenseless men, women, and children at places like Camp Grant, Sand Creek, and Wounded Knee. They confined thousands of Indians on reservations seemingly like concentration camps. And all the while they were doing this to the Indians, who had now lost their power, the nation largely turned its attention to other matters.

But to some Americans in these same years the spirit of 1776 lived on. And in the post-Civil War generation there were men and women who worked to maintain the ideal of freedom so that the blessings of liberty and the promises of democracy would be shared by all Americans regardless of the color of their skin. One such American at this time of great tribulation for the Indian was Helen Hunt Jackson (1830–1885) who was to arouse the national conscience of her day about the sufferings and maltreatment of the first Americans. She had pledged to do this. And within a period of four years before her death in 1885, in her severe arraignment of federal Indian policy in A Century of Dishonor (1881) and her sentimental novel, Ramona (1884), Mrs. Jackson awakened the nation to the plight of the Indians.

Her books caused a national sensation, and she became one of the most influential persons in the late nineteenth century to call public attention to the Indian problem and one of the most effective writers of those years in behalf of better treatment of the Indians. After the appearance of her books and her crusade it was no longer possible for the nation to continue to ignore and to neglect the long-suffering Indians. Just a few days before she died, she wrote to President Grover Cleveland asking him to read her *Century of Dishonor* and saying, "I am dying happier for the belief I have that it is your hand that is destined to strike the first steady blow toward lifting this burden of infamy from our country and righting the wrongs of the Indian race."

Helen Hunt Jackson's *A Century of Dishonor* became the classic account of American injustice to the Indian and has remained so. It is a powerful story of dispossession, broken treaties, crooked dealings, promises not kept, and inhumane treatment on the part of the federal government toward a number of important Indian tribes who were by now its powerless wards. "All the heart and soul I possess have gone into it," she wrote, and this is so. It is an emotional and partisan book and is not balanced history, but it could hardly be otherwise, because it is an impassioned plea to the country to rectify its policy of mistreating the Indians. It was not only aimed at stirring up the public conscience of the day but was also directed toward Congress with the hope this body would do something on behalf of Indian rights. Mrs. Jackson, at her own expense, sent a copy to every member of Congress with the following words printed in red on the cover: "Look upon your hands! They are stained with the blood of your relations."

There were other books at the same time attacking federal Indian policy and calling for its reform, but none had the same stunning effect upon the public as *A Century of Dishonor*. Indeed, its impact was so great, it has been called the *Uncle Tom's Cabin* of the Indians's cause. And Mrs. Jackson regarded herself as an "Indian Harriet Beecher Stowe," about whom she wrote: "If I can do one-hundreth part for the Indians as Mrs. Stowe did for the Negro, I will be thankful." While some contemporaries and subsequent historians criticized Mrs. Jackson for overstating her case and not giving a fair appraisal of the Indian problem, no one could ignore the powerful message she set forth. And as one of the modern historians of the American Indian writes about her: "Critics have damned her lack of balance, even suppression of facts that did not fit her preconceptions, but in *A Century of Dishonor* and *Ramona* she publicized the Indian cause as it had never been publicized before."

77

It was not until late in her life that Mrs. Jackson became a champion of Indian rights. For most of her previous years she had followed such pursuits as those of a housewife, a poet, and a novelist. Then in 1879, near the end of her life, she became converted to Indian reforms after hearing the Ponca chieftain Standing Bear tell about the sufferings of the Plains Indians. Almost at once she began to champion the cause of these Indians. Not only did she expose the story of governmental mistreatment of the Indians in her books, but she sent out petitions, wrote letters to newspapers, and endeavored to stir up public opinion on behalf of the Indians. Soon she was a reformer and was at war with government officials over their Indian policy.

Once Mrs. Jackson had presented the case against the government for its failure to protect and to look after the Indians, later reformers could only repeat what she had said. And the Indian reform movement owed much to her. Within a year after the publication of *A Century of Dishonor,* the Indian Rights Association was created. And one of the country's most prominent historians, Allan Nevins, who believed Mrs. Jackson was a sentimentalist who had overstated her case, also concluded, "the general agitation in which she played so prominent a part was largely responsible for the enactment in 1887 of the Dawes Act, the first comprehensive, constructive and altogether wise piece of legislation for the advancement of the Indians." This law initiated a new Indian policy reversing the old military policy of extermination. The Act gave land directly to individual Indians and provided for the dissolution of tribal autonomy. It also allowed Indians to receive full United States citizenship.

In spite of the Dawes Act and the good intentions behind it, the new policy did not work well. It subsequently was revised several times, and the plight of the Indians still remains on our national conscience. Helen Hunt Jackson pricked that conscience in her day by showing clearly how the federal government ignored and mistreated the Indians who deserved to share in the blessings of liberty and the promises of democracy as every other American. Hope of something being done for the Indians never died in her heart. As Allan Nevins writes, "We can point to her as eloquent evidence that at one period in our history a large body of Americans began to care, a large body began to be ashamed."

Why did Helen Hunt Jackson champion the cause of the Indians? Some of her contemporaries believed her books were spiteful diatribes and capable of doing much harm. But she labored in behalf of Indians to improve their conditions and to protect their rights in the spirit of 1776, because this was her understanding of that spirit.

Jane Addams

ALLEN F. DAVIS

Jane Addams was born in a little town in northern Illinois on the eve of the Civil War, but like so many of her generation she left the small town and moved to the city. Jane Addams tried to confront the massive problems which industrialism, urbanization, and immigration had brought to America—problems which threatened the very existence of the democratic form of government established by the founding fathers. The new country, begun in 1789 by the revolutionary generation, was a small, rural nation consisting of less than three million people, the great majority of English origin, living on the east coast of North America. Philadelphia with slightly less than 25,000 people in 1776 was the largest city in the colonies. By 1900 New York City had a population of three and a half million (more than the rest of the country in 1790) and Chicago and Philadelphia were not far behind. The country sprawled from the Atlantic to the Pacific and every year from 1900 to 1914 saw an average of nearly a million new immigrants arrive in the United States. How these people, many with little knowledge of American language and customs, could still have the freedom and opportunity envisioned for all Americans by the founding fathers was the challenge taken up by Jane Addams. She was also especially concerned that women, facing the new problems of urban America, be given equal opportunities and roles.

Jane Addams's decision to move to the slums of Chicago and found a social settlement, which she called Hull House, did not come easily. She was the daughter of a prosperous miller and businessman, and she grew up in an era when it was assumed that girls would become wives and mothers and ladies, while the more active and important work of the world was left to the men. But Jane Addams wanted to become a doctor or a scientist, and like a few other women of her generation, she broke with tradition and went to college. But there were few careers open even to women college graduates in the 1880s. One could become a school teacher or perhaps a missionary but neither appealed to Jane Addams, and like all of her contemporaries she assumed that a woman could not combine marriage with a career. She did enter medical school, but had to drop out because of failing health. Then for eight years she floundered. She traveled for extended periods in Europe; she played the role of maiden aunt while caring for her sister's children. She studied and she waited. Then while visiting London in 1888 with Ellen Starr, a former college friend, she discovered Toynbee Hall, the first social settlement, and in the process she found a way to help the urban poor while also providing useful and important careers for a growing number of well-educated men and women.

Hull House, which opened in Chicago in 1889 was not the first social settlement in America but it quickly became the most famous. The basic idea was for a group of well-educated men and women to live in a crowded, working-class neighborhood. They came to teach and to share, but they also came to learn from the people living there, for they felt that their backgrounds and education had cut them off from the reality of American life. They also sought to build bridges and lines of communications across the class and ethnic divisions which they saw developing in America.

Jane Addams had only a vague idea how she might help the poor and begin to solve the problems of urban America when she moved to the west side of Chicago, but she was willing to learn and Hull House quickly attracted a group of able and dedicated people, especially talented and energetic women, who, like Jane Addams, were seeking something useful to do. Florence Kelley, the daughter of a Philadelphia congressman and judge, had been educated at Cornell and the University of Zurich. A powerful and able person she became the country's leading expert on child labor reform and secretary of the National Consumer's League. Julia Lathrop was more retiring in personality than Florence Kelley but just as able. She helped to organize the first juvenile court, the Immigrants Protective League, and in 1912 became the first head of the Children's Bureau. Ellen Starr, the co-founder, was interested in art, and she ran a bookbindery but she also was an ardent defender of organized labor and joined the picket line at the least provocation. Alice Hamilton, a petite woman with an M.D., became an authority on industrial medicine and the first woman professor at Harvard Medical School. Grace and Edith Abbott, sisters from Nebraska, were also Hull House residents and leading experts on the city and its problems. Edith became dean of the School of Social Service Administration at the University of Chicago and Grace was director of the Immigrant Protective League and then head of the Children's Bureau. There were many others, for Hull House became a training ground for a new generation of professional women and urban experts, and it was also an outpost in the slums where campaigns were launched to improve urban living. Over it all presided Jane Addams, a shrewd business woman and an excellent organizer. She was always calm and serene and as much at home on the lecture platform as she was talking to an immigrant neighbor near Hull House.

During the first winter at Hull House the settlement workers tried to give Christmas candy to the children in the neighborhood. They were surprised when the children refused, until they learned that these children worked twelve hours a day, six days a week in a candy factory. They also discovered other children in the neighborhood who had been stunted mentally and physically or permanently injured because they were forced to work in factories at eight or ten or twelve years of age. The Hull House group vowed to wipe out child labor. They investigated, wrote reports, and lobbied for the passage of state laws. Eventually they worked to pass federal laws which did eliminate some of the worst abuses, but they discovered that any change came very slowly and sometimes the same battle had to be fought over and over again.

The settlement workers were especially concerned with the dirty streets and unhealthy conditions in their neighborhood. Slaughter houses, fish peddlers, livery stables (as well as ordinary citizens) dumped refuse into the streets which became a sea of mud in the spring and fall and a duststorm in the summer. Garbage was rarely collected in the district which aggravated the problem, so Jane Addams submitted a bid for the garbage contract in the ward. Her bid was thrown out on a technicality, but the publicity it received did prompt the mayor to appoint her a garbage inspector. For several weeks Jane Addams and her immaculately dressed women assistants could be seen at six o'clock in the morning walking behind the horse drawn garbage truck as it made its rounds in the neighborhood. But the settlement workers quickly learned that to solve a local problem they usually had to go to city hall, the state house, and often to Washington. Yet they continued to work to improve life in the cities, and many of their innovations were taken over by other organizations.

Jane Addams and her co-workers, responding to the needs they saw around them, opened a kindergarten, an art gallery, and an apartment for working girls. They built a gymnasium, an arts and crafts shop, a music school, and they began classes in English for the immigrant neighbors. The settlement which had begun as one small building in 1889 grew to include thirteen buildings which covered more than a city block in 1907. The settlement workers tried to improve the condition of housing in the city, to open more parks and playgrounds, and to make the schools more responsive to the needs of their neighbors. They had the optimistic view that if a person could have a good house to live in and a good school to go to he could become a better person. They made surveys, wrote reports, articles and books. They testified before committees and made speeches. Jane Addams alone wrote 10 books and 400 articles. In the process they began to educate the American people about the realities of life in an urban environment, and they helped to change American attitudes toward poverty. Most people, they argued, were poor not because they were lazy or sinful or unfit, but because of the social environment in which they lived. The message was clear: change the environment and eliminate poverty.

Jane Addams was especially concerned with the harsh process of Americanization which she witnessed in her neighborhood. She saw young people from foreign countries totally reject the customs, language, and often the religion of their parents and grandparents. She appreciated the need to preserve the customs, the handicrafts and festivals of each immigrant group. She also grasped the need for young people to feel pride in their parents and in their heritage. She taught that one did not have to cease being Irish or Italian or Greek to become an American and that one did not have to reject a relative simply because he spoke strangely and wore different clothes. Diversity not uniformity was the strength of America.

Jane Addams also worked hard to promote equal opportunity for women. She campaigned for women suffrage, but unlike some advocates she argued for the vote for immigrant and lower class women. She maintained that women, because of their traditional role of housekeepers, had special qualifications to become involved in municipal housekeeping. Clean streets, a good water supply, an efficient government directly affected the health of women and their families and they ought to have a voice in selecting their leaders. Jane Addams's efforts to help women did not stop with the vote; she worked to promote laws to safeguard women in industry and to provide equal opportunities in education, government and in the labor movement. Perhaps most of all, by lecturing, writing books and actively participating in reform campaigns she provided an example of what a woman could do for millions of young women.

During and after World War I, Jane Addams spent a large part of her time and energy working for the Women's International League for Peace and Freedom and trying to promote international understanding. Her experience in a neighborhood where eighteen ethnic groups lived convinced her of the possibility and the need for cooperation and sharing among nations.

Jane Addams's crusade to improve life in the cities of America and to promote peace in the world did not achieve any easy victories. Many of the problems she faced still remain unsolved today, but she truly represented the best of the spirit of 1776. She was in the words of William Allen White an example of "the altruistic element in a civilization that on the whole is too acquisitive."

John Dewey

VINCENT P. LANNIE

A greying and distinguished man opened heavy oak doors, walked through dark corridors, and entered a typical American schoolroom of the 1890s. He saw rows of ugly desks placed in geometrical order and crowded together with just enough space for children to move uncomfortably through the aisles. The desks were all the same size and could hold no more than a few books, pencils, and paper. These were "listening desks," observed the visitor, for "simply studying lessons out of a book is only

87

another kind of listening." Passivity, the mere rote absorption of ready-made and teacher-prepared materials, was the only type of instruction possible in such a classroom. The treatment of each child as a separate individual seemed utopian; and the total school environment projected an atmosphere of dealing with youngsters as collective numbers and units. Such a system of education was repulsive to John Dewey (1859–1952) who had just been appointed to head the Department of Philosophy, Psychology, and Pedagogy at the University of Chicago.

Schoolrooms had not always been so depressing. America's founding fathers could not fathom a nation both free and ignorant; and Thomas Jefferson considered education as the most effective antidote to tyranny and violence. In the new Republic every man was a king and every man had the right to participate in the leadership decisions affecting the total citizenry. Yet it was not every man but every educated man who could fulfill these civic responsibilities. Education, therefore, made the difference between advanced and backward nations. As with nations, so too with individuals.

It took another generation before Americans decided upon the public or common school as the best institution to fulfill the nation's educational needs. It was public because it was established and supported by the state, open to all children on an equal basis, and "subject to such inspection as the law may institute." It was common "because it is the debt which the community owes to every citizen for their good and its security." Such a school would cut across social, religious, and economic differences and provide a common educational experience for all youngsters. Horace Mann, Henry Barnard, and other pre-Civil War educators viewed this newly emerging school as a panacea for social ills, "the great equalizer of the condition of men," and the salvation of American democracy.

Nearly fifty years had passed since the nation's schools reaped the benefits of Horace Mann's common school crusade. By the turn of the twentieth century America had taken a quantum leap forward as technology, capital investment, and scientific discoveries transformed a once divided country into a major world power. Of all the changes that occurred in the United States, the most important was the industrial one. Such a change was not only national but international in scope and nothing short of a revolution. A vast system of manufacturing mushroomed to supply an ever-expanding national and world market as cheaper and more rapid means of communication and distribution were in the process of development. Within this transformation of American society, everything seemed to be in a state of flux. Cities attracted millions of persons, immigrants as well as rural Americans. A hideous conglomeration of hunger, vice, disease, and crime unfortunately arose and turned large parts of many cities into ghettos of gloom and despair.

The schools were no better and projected a similar depressing picture. Rural schools remained ungraded and poorly taught with untrained teachers routinely drilling pupils in the McGuffey Readers. In the cities school buildings, already obsolete, badly lighted, inadequately heated, and frequently unsanitary, were bursting at the seams as thousands of immigrant and newly-arrived farm children teemed into classrooms. Instruction was at best mediocre; and at times degenerated to the level of the Chicago teacher who, conducting a "concert drill," ordered her pupils: "Don't stop to think, tell me what you know!" All across the land citizens complained that the schools did not meet the needs of rural or urban youth. They were too book-oriented and even this "intellectual" education was more often than not "singsong drill, rote repetition, and meaningless verbiage." Youngsters left school as soon as they could and many of them never completed the eighth grade. Public education was on the spot. The time was right for a new breed of educational reformer to appear on the scene.

John Dewey was such a person. Blessed with a long life of over ninety years, he personally witnessed the advance of post-Civil War America into a leading industrial nation. A New Englander by birth and a philosopher by training, he received an early Ph.D. from Johns Hopkins University. In 1884 he joined the University of Michigan faculty and eventually participated in the state's teacher education program for high schools. Ten years later he left for the University of Chicago where he and his wife established a laboratory school which emerged as an important testing center for his educational theories. In 1904 he accepted a professorship in philosophy at Columbia University and lectured regularly on pedagogical subjects at the University's Teachers College. He remained there until retirement in 1930, though he continued to speak and write on American education for another score of years.

Early in his career Dewey judged that American education had become a symbol of passive inactivity. The schoolroom had become synonymous with the mechanical massing of children and a curriculum often irrelevant to the world of the young. Uniformity of method and textbook placed the center of educational gravity outside the child. All served to "pour in" and nothing served to "draw out." Such an education was antithetical to Dewey's conception of a democracy. For in his view education was the indispensable criterion for the success of American democracy.

Dewey believed that democracy was cut from the very fabric of the American experience. It was vital to the free interaction of groups in a society—to the extent that such groups shared common interests. Such a society exempted nothing from examination and alteration or even possible reconstruction. Change was nothing more than the opportunity to rebuild society along more just and humane standards. Yet no set of absolute truths ruled social change nor was a democracy automatically directed toward preconceived and eternal goals. Human intelligence constituted the source for social values and ethics while the collective populace undergirded all moral authority in such a society. In a penetrating insight, Dewey argued that a democracy was not fundamentally a form of government but "primarily a mode of associated living, of conjoint communicated experience." Thus a democracy was a way of life profoundly influencing community goals and individual desires. It embraced not only political and governmental concerns but all institutional structures, mores, and artistic impulses of a society.

A democratic society demanded a democratic education—an education that balanced the needs of society with the needs of each individual in that society. Dewey never minimized the importance of individuals; and in *The Child and the Curriculum* (1902) he emphasized the child as the center of his educational thought and a curriculum based on experience as the foundation stones of a democratic education. He posited four instincts of a child—interest in communication, inquiry, construction, and artistic expression—and maintained that they were the natural resources upon which depended the active growth of the child. Growth led to growth, that is, education remained a life-long process, and thus nothing was alien to the school.

But Dewey always focused his major attention upon the societal aspects of a democratic education. If democracy was more than a governmental mode, then a democratic education was more than memorizing a predetermined number of facts and tables. If democracy was "a mode of associated living," then a democratic education was a "reconstruction or reorganization of experience which adds to the meaning of experience, and which increases ability to direct the course of subsequent experience." In one of his earliest books, *The School and Society* (1899), Dewey challenged the public school to reflect the larger American society by transcending its traditional isolation and assume a central role in the struggle for a better life. In this view, the school would become an "embryonic community" reflecting the life of the larger society. This meant an open curriculum that extended beyond historical preoccupation with language and literature to an inclusion of scientific and industrial studies concerned with the vast panorama of human affairs. In his mind the school thus emerged as the central institution of American democracy. It worked out social problems on an experimental basis, using at appropriate times organized subject matter, adult direction and guidance, and the role of the past. In Dewey's masterpiece, *Democracy and Education* (1916), he drew out many of the implications of the integral relationship of education to a democratic society first proposed in *The School and Society* seventeen years earlier. Ultimately, he believed that democracy would be fostered only as schooling became popularized in character and in clientele. Only in this way could the American way of life mature into a society that was "worthy, lovely, and harmonious." And unless every person capably and freely participated in such a society, then Dewey questioned its very existence.

In time Dewey achieved recognition as the leading progressive educator of the twentieth century. In the years between the two world wars, progressive education made great strides on the American scene. It embraced public and private schools, and touched every aspect of the educational ladder from the elementary school through the university.

Yet the older Dewey became, the more he appeared as a "reverently misinterpreted prophet rather than a carefully obeyed commander." Would-be followers misunderstood and vulgarized his thought; and such terms as life adjustment, permissiveness, antiintellectualism, and antiauthoritarianism often became synonymous with progressive education. *Auntie Mame* sent her nephew Patrick to a "progressive" school in the 1920s where boys and girls stripped to understand the particularities of male and female fish! Nowhere was progressive education more pungently caricatured than in the cartoon of a school with a caption which had the children bemoan: "Do we have to do what we want to do?"

Following World War II critics of progressive education charged the schools with being intellectually mediocre and "coddling" too many youngsters. In the "cold war" era, Russian scientific progress, most threateningly symbolized by the launching of Sputnik in 1957, loomed as a serious challenge to American power and prestige. The country could not afford to lose the battle, and strident voices called for the intellectual improvement of the schools. Such works as Albert Lynd's *Quackery in the Public Schools*, Arthur Bestor's *Educational Wasteland*, Robert Hutchins's *Let's Talk Sense About Our Schools*, and Paul Woodring's *The Diminished Mind* severely criticized progressive education on the elementary and secondary levels. In a more moderate tone, James B. Conant, former president of Harvard University, wrote a series of volumes—*The American High School, Slums and Suburbs*, and *The American Junior High School*—which defended the basic structure of American education though recommending a series of immediate reforms.

Yet none of these critics challenged Dewey's contention about the centrality of public education in a democratic society. Neither did the civil rights movement of the 1960s which urged the schools to achieve equality for all children irrespective of color. The schoolbus controversy of the 1970s further involved the schools in the quest for a more perfect democratic society.

But the 1970s witnessed the rise of neo-romanticism upon the American educational scene—a view that categorically and emphatically rejected Dewey's contention concerning the centrality of schooling in a democratic society. Voices such as Ivan Illich and John Holt argued that the schools stilted the creative minds of the young and called for the deschooling of American society. Until recently the school was called upon to be all things to all men. Now new thinkers challenged the very need for schooling in a democracy, pleading for alternative forms of education. For the first time in over a century, the school was asked to take a back seat in fostering American democracy.

Dewey would reproach none of his critics. A democracy must always be in a state of fluid change and education must constantly reinterpret new experience. To this creed Dewey remained committed to the end. And for him an end was but a prelude to a beginning.

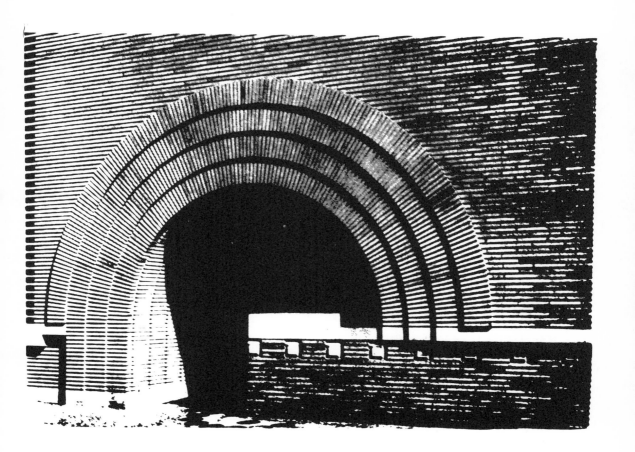

Frank Lloyd Wright

WILBERT R. HASBROUCK

Within a radius of a few hundred miles from the southern tip of Lake Michigan, there is more great architecture standing than in any other area of similar size in the world.

Midwestern America is the cradle of the development of modern architecture. It is, moreover, the birthplace of the practice of architecture as we know it today. It was into this environment that Frank Lloyd Wright was born in 1867.

95

There is no question that the geography of the area played a large part in the needs which brought about the buildings which are acknowledged as the forerunners of the skyscrapers and residences of today. The major transportation routes to the west during the mid-nineteenth century passed through northern Indiana to the area now occupied by metropolitan Chicago where, like the spokes of a giant wheel, men and materials radiated to the west, south and north while the products of their labors returned to the markets in the east. Thus Indiana became a part of this great development and her western boundary, an artificial barrier defined only by a line on a map rather than by natural obstacles, did nothing to prevent the ferment of early development in architecture and other cultural events from enriching her heritage.

The Chicago fire of 1871 caused the infant profession of architecture to mature overnight. Buildings were needed by the thousands, and engineers, architects, builders and men of forethought supplied that need. No longer could the skilled carpenter or stonemason act as the masterbuilder who designed as well as built to satisfy his patron. The events of the latter half of the 19th century were moving too fast to permit one man to do all. It became mandatory that architects prepare complete detailed drawings of complex structures prior to construction. Thus, the profession was radically revised in the span of only a few years.

A few individuals stand out as prime examples in the movement toward a modern operation which became architecture as we know it. William Le Baron Jenney, formerly an officer with the Union Army and trained as an engineer, turned his talents towards building the commercial structures so desperately needed by the businessmen in Chicago who served as brokers to the West and suppliers of raw materials to their eastern counterparts. Joseph Lyman Silsbee, steeped in the traditional architecture of the East came to the Midwest to design churches, small commercial structures, and residences for the wealthy. The drafting boards of his office spawned the germ of a new residential architecture. From these two offices the great firms of the early twentieth century as well as many of those today can largely trace their ancestry. Jenney's office served as a classroom for Louis Sullivan, the man who later revolutionized the construction and philosophy of the tall building. Frank Lloyd Wright first found work in the office of Silsbee where for just over a year he learned the basics of his craft. Sullivan left Jenney to complete his education in Europe and then, returning to Chicago, he joined Dankmar Adler where he eventually became a partner. When the office of Adler and Sullivan became too busy for Sullivan to handle all aspects of design, he brought young Frank Lloyd Wright into the firm, first as a draftsman of ornament in 1887 and, later, to act as chief draftsman. Wright became Sullivan's right hand. He also became Sullivan's friend and confidant. Sullivan recognized the great social changes taking place during Wright's tenure in his office and he never tired of talking with his young assistant. He conveyed his philosophy of architecture to Wright, a philosophy so broad as to encompass all building. Wright absorbed it all.

The office was at its peak during the six years Wright was with Sullivan. Both Adler and Sullivan were so involved with their clients for commercial structures that they had little time for smaller commissions, particularly residences. It fell to their young designer, Frank Lloyd Wright, to handle those clients who could not, for various reasons, be refused. Thus it was Wright who generally carried out the residential commissions for the office of Adler and Sullivan. His training in Silsbee's office stood him in good stead and the principles so carefully instilled by his *Lieber Meister*, Louis Sullivan, were not forgotten as they were incorporated into the work he did for all. Eventually, Wright began taking private clients which precipitated a quarrel that led to his leaving Adler and Sullivan. When he left, he took with him an education in architecture which no other architect ever had before or will have again. He established his own office and began a career which spanned more than seventy-five years.

The work of Frank Lloyd Wright is located in nearly every one of these United States. Illinois can boast the largest number of Wright's completed works with Michigan close behind. Indiana has the benefit of five of Wright's finished buildings which span a total of almost fifty years and represent three distinct periods of his creativity. More important, Wright's impact on the architecture of Indiana has been felt since the earliest of his works was completed and continues to be a part of the architectural scene today.

Frank Lloyd Wright was responsible for the "Prairie School" of architecture. This school, really a style of its own, can be characterized as being an architecture particularly suited to low, rolling prairies accented by native trees of the Midwest. Certain materials and ornamental elements make these early Wright buildings easily recognizable. Much later in his life, beginning in the 1930s, Wright began a new approach to residential

97

building. He designed a basic plan consisting of essentially a living-work area with a wing of sleeping rooms all on a single level. This plan, which he called the "Usonian" house was subject to great variation but the basic design remained. It, too, is easily recognizable by student and layman alike.

In 1906 Frank Lloyd Wright built the K. C. De Rhodes house in South Bend, Indiana. Forty-two years later he built another building in South Bend for the Herman T. Mossberg family. The De Rhodes house represents a prime example of the best of Wright's "Prairie" houses. It typifies what Wright was doing in the first decade of the twentieth century. It is built on a cruciform plan, has a stucco exterior with wood trim, and contains all of the basic elements which Wright made famous in his early period. It is still standing today, albeit somewhat altered and no longer a residence. The Mossberg house is also standing in mint condition and still a superb example of Wright's Usonian architecture. The Usonian houses of Wright have undoubtedly been the single most influential element in the maturing of modern single family residential architecture in the world. The long low lines of the Mossberg house with its horizontal siding combined with brick and glass typify Wright's work but also typify the best work of a quarter century of "new towns" built following World War II.

Wright's other work in Indiana includes the Armstrong house on the south shore of Lake Michigan which was built in 1938. This house, an earlier example of the Usonian house, stands as a testament to the genius of Wright in the development of the low cost house which was so much in demand during the depression years of the 1930s. It, too, has its progeny in the "new towns" of the last quarter century. The other two buildings in Indiana by the hand of Frank Lloyd Wright were those for the Davis family in Marion, completed in 1950 and the house in West Lafayette built for the Christian family in 1954. These last two homes were done in the heyday of Wright's last great creative work. They represent, as well as any houses Wright ever did, a culmination of the thought his mind brought to architecture, particularly that of homes, over several generations of practice.

Wright was a master architect. He has been called the father of the "Prairie" school. He was, of course, just that. We must keep in mind, however, that a single man does not constitute a "school of architecture." He was the foundation, the fountainhead, the inspiration of many who were to follow him. Wright's impact on the architectural world was enormous. It was not lost in Indiana.

Wright's early work was closely watched by his colleagues in the Hoosier state. The observers were many, the men who understood him numbered somewhat fewer. Those who did understand were able to give a splendid accounting of themselves and their work. South Bend's two buildings by Wright had and still have, their admirers. The De Rhodes house in particular influenced architects and architecture in Indiana to a degree seldom realized today. Most notable is the work of two men, N. Roy Shambleau and Ernest W. Young.

Young and Shambleau both began practice in Indiana prior to Wright's first work in the state. Both built numerous residential structures in the Prairie style prior to the first World War. Young's early works included the Eberhart house at 402 Lincoln Way East, Mishawaka, now remodeled into offices, the Talcott house in South Bend at 1901 Riverside Drive and at least a dozen others still standing. His own house, also located in South Bend, was built in the Prairie style at 1216 Hillcrest Road.

Roy Shambleau's commission included a splendid Prairie house for the Keightly family in South Bend. Oddly enough, this house first was built on Jefferson Street and later moved to its present location at 1027 East Wayne. Shambleau built a number of other houses in the Prairie style in and around South Bend.

Both Young and Shambleau extended their influence beyond their executed buildings by teaching architecture at the University of Notre Dame. Furthermore, they combined efforts to publish, for a short time, a monthly journal titled *Unique Homes*. Featuring their own Prairie designs, their influence on other architects and builders by this means can only be speculated.

Following the First World War, Wright's influence became even more evident with the advent of the work of Barry Byrne in Indiana. Byrne, often noted as Wright's most successful disciple, built the J. B. Franke house in Fort Wayne, Indiana. It is basically derivative of the work of Frank Lloyd Wright but Byrne had by this time developed an architecture of his own. The interior in particular shows Byrne's own understanding of Prairie architecture. In many ways, Byrne, in this single commission, represents Wright's greatest accomplishment. That is, Byrne took his experience with Wright and developed his own interpretation of the Prairie School. From his hands came not a copy but a superb interpretation of the architecture

99

first developed by Frank Lloyd Wright for the prairies of the Midwest so evident in the state of Indiana.

As we celebrate our bicentennial year, we can find but a few names of persons who truly exemplify both centuries of our country's life. Frank Lloyd Wright is one of those few. Born into pre-Victorian America in 1867 just two years after the Civil War, he lived for nearly ninety-two years. Of those years, almost three quarters of a century were spent in active architectural practice. Wright's roots were always in the Victorian era of his youth while his architecture became the dominant influence on American life and culture in the twentieth century.

There is no doubt that Frank Lloyd Wright succeeded in his probably apocryphal goal of becoming "the greatest architect of all time." Indiana, in the heart of Wright's beloved Midwest, is fortunate to have both the work of the master and standing evidence of his legacy to modern architecture as well.

"Those who won our independence
believed that the final end of
the state was to make men free
to develop their faculties;
and that in its government the
deliberative forces should pre-
vail over the arbitrary. They
valued liberty both as an end
and as a means. They believed
liberty to be the secret of
happiness and courage to be
the secret of liberty."

Louis D. Brandeis

STANLEY I. KUTLER

Louis Dembitz Brandeis (1856–1941) reflected the spirit of the American Revolution as did few other public servants in twentieth century American life. That spirit offered the American people independence, opportunity, and freedom. It fostered the idea of a government of laws to create an environment for people to realize their individual creative capacities for the common good; and yet, a government so restrained as not to impair the fundamental liberties of any individual whatever the demands of the larger society. In his capacity as the "People's Attorney" and as an associate justice of the United States Supreme Court, Brandeis consistently devoted himself to the preservation of those "unalienable rights" of "life, liberty, and the pursuit of happiness." His own life involved a constant search for personal, economic, and intellectual freedom, and his public efforts represented a commitment to the attainment of the same freedoms for all Americans.

Brandeis was born on November 13, 1856, in Louisville, Kentucky. His parents had migrated from Bohemia as part of that political group of emigrees known as the "Forty-eighters" who fled Europe after the failure of the liberal revolutions of 1848. The Brandeis family's Jewish heritage and concern for social justice significantly influenced the political and social ideas of the future jurist.

Brandeis attended public schools in Louisville, studied two years in Europe, and received a law degree from Harvard in 1877. After a brief period in a St. Louis law office, he returned to Boston in 1879 where he developed a distinguished corporate law practice. Beginning in the 1890s, however, Brandeis increasingly worked for consumer and public causes. For example, he exposed abuses in gas, railroad, and insurance rates, and in this capacity he arrayed himself against some of the most formidable private enterprises. Brandeis relied upon facts to refute the extravagant claims of private business firms and their tyrannical abuse of the public interest. In these battles, Brandeis usually served without fee, earning the title, the "People's Attorney." "I shall be glad," he told Clarence Darrow, "to give such assistance as I can and shall want no compensation other than the satisfaction of having aided a good cause."

Brandeis identified with a wide variety of progressive reforms, beginning with his criticism of Boston subway rates in the 1890s, and continuing with statewide and national activities in behalf of workmen's compensation, labor rights, consumer protection, and conservation. Whatever the particular object, Brandeis unrelentingly focused on the abusive, intimidating force of monopoly power. His activities soon led him into national politics, first as an adviser to Senator Robert M. La Follette and then to Woodrow Wilson during the campaign of 1912. Powerful interests and individuals persuaded Wilson not to appoint Brandeis as attorney general. Privately, Brandeis continued to counsel Wilson, and he played a prominent role in shaping such major legislation as the Federal Reserve and the Clayton Antitrust Acts.

In 1916, Wilson nominated Brandeis for a seat on the Supreme Court. The selection stirred powerful antagonism; seven past presidents of the American Bar Association attacked Brandeis as "not a fit person" to serve. Brandeis's public service activities, as well as his Jewish background, had created powerful enemies who nearly succeeded in blocking the nomination. After protracted hearings lasting nearly five months, the Senate confirmed Brandeis's nomination and he served with distinction until his retirement in 1939.

Americans rebelled in 1776 because they believed that the British government had failed in its obligation to protect their rights as Englishmen. They also were convinced that British imperial authorities no longer provided a government flexible enough to satisfy the changing needs and demands of American society. Throughout his long judicial tenure, Brandeis devoted himself to rationalizing and supporting the idea of a positive government that would constantly serve those ever-evolving social and economic needs. During many of those years, the Supreme Court often thwarted efforts of the state and national governments to regulate economic forces that dominated or affected people's lives. Brandeis, along with colleagues such as Oliver Wendell Holmes, Harlan Fiske Stone, and Benjamin N. Cardozo, supported governmental regulation of corporate trusts, working conditions, and public utility rates, for example. For many years, Brandeis found himself in a minority, yet he lived to see most of his dissenting views become law. Ever responsive to the ideal of achieving a better society, Brandeis believed in "the fundamental right of free men to strive for better conditions through new legislation and new institutions."

Throughout his career, Brandeis resisted the notion that it was the Court's function to strike down legislative experiments because the laws offended the justices' own economic biases or their static view of the Constitution. For him, part of the meaning of a free society meant the freedom "to remould, through experimentation, our economic practices and institutions to meet changing social and economic needs." While he acknowledged that the Court could prevent such experiments, he admonished his colleagues that "we must be ever on our guard, lest we erect our prejudices into legal principles. If we would guide by the light of reason, we must let our minds be bold."

Yet, like those who had shaped the American Revolution. Brandeis recognized that government had the capacity for mischief, as well as good. Just as he distrusted the concentration of excessive economic power, Brandeis was ever vigilant of the potential of big government to abuse the rights of individuals. In 1928, for example, in the first government wiretap case heard by the Court, Brandeis vigorously opposed the indiscriminate use of such power by the government, even if necessary to enforce a valid law. In this case, government agents had tapped the telephones of men suspected of violating the prohibition laws. Although Brandeis supported the "noble experiment," he could not condone the prohibition bureau's indiscriminate invasion of individual privacy. In one of his most prophetic opinions, he warned against rationalizing dubious means for desirable ends. "Our government," Brandeis wrote, "is the potent, the omnipresent teacher. For good or ill, it teaches the whole people by example. Crime is contagious. If the government becomes a lawbreaker, it breeds contempt for law; it invites every man to become a law unto himself; it invites anarchy. To declare that in the administration of the criminal law the end justifies the means—to declare that the government may commit crimes in order to secure the conviction of a private criminal—would bring terrible retribution."

The preservation of law and order indeed is the responsibility of government; yet men who govern must themselves be mindful of the law. Two hundred years after the American Revolution, the American people still confront government that would threaten their liberty in the name of law and order or national security. However attractive the government's purpose might be, Brandeis warned that "experience should teach us to be most on our guard to protect liberty when the government's purposes are beneficent. Men born to freedom are naturally alert to repel invasion of their liberty by evil-minded rulers. The greatest dangers to liberty lurk in insidious encroachment by men of zeal, well-meaning, but without understanding."

For the purpose of preserving an open society, Brandeis referred directly to the spirit of 1776. "Those who won our independence by revolution were not cowards," he wrote in 1927. "They did not exalt order at the cost of liberty." The rights of dissent and free political debate, he held, were essential for a nation that treasured its liberty. With "those who won our independence," Brandeis believed "liberty to be the secret of happiness and courage to be the secret of liberty." A repressive, arbitrary state was not one in which deliberative forces could operate in order to realize the true end and purpose of the state—"to make men free to develop their faculties."

Brandeis directed his judicial efforts to the principle that "our Constitution undertook to secure conditions favorable to the pursuit of happiness." Happiness in the context of the American Revolution encompassed both material and spiritual goals that would make society free and secure. He conducted himself in that fashion and devoted himself to the task of educating and helping others to the same goals. Liberty involves the corollary acceptance of responsibility, and Brandeis insisted that freedom also entailed a sense of obligation to the community. As a young student, he recorded this principle, one which continually governed his own life: "Republics are not ungrateful, but the debt of each citizen to his country is so great that no payments, however large, can extinguish it."

Brandeis's commitment to achieving a better society and expanded freedom carried him into an enormous range of efforts: as lawyer, legal scholar (with his pioneering essay, "The Right to Privacy" in 1890), urban reformer, presidential adviser, Zionist, and jurist. In all, he was remarkably consistent in thought and action. His reform commitments did not stem from psychological frustrations whereby the outsider finds himself alienated from things as they are. Rather, they involved a genuine devotion to the political and economic system as it was supposed to be. Reform for him always transcended immediate considerations as he geared his efforts toward stimulating individual creativity and freeing the individual from impersonal, oppressive restraints. His interests in lower, equitable gas rates in Boston and a Jewish National Home thus were not dissimilar.

In a sense, Brandeis and other reformers won many of their battles, yet lost the war. Despite the crusades against bigness, we remain the children of Leviathan. Ironically, we treasure the reform cycles of the twentieth century that did so much to expand the scope and activities of government. But where have we gone? Corporate power, despite all the regulatory devices, often operates irresponsibly. Monopoly practice—now labor as well as capital—still dominates the economic system; we have not established a genuinely competitive system, as Brandeis had hoped. More important, we have found that a reliance upon government often defeats the very purposes of reform. We have substituted impersonal, faceless public institutions and bureaucracies for private ones, but it is doubtful whether they have served the public interest any better.

The excessive expansion and abuses of governmental power today are legion. The Watergate and CIA revelations have made Brandeis's observations about "beneficent" governmental purposes ever more pertinent. Unlike many of his worshipful disciples, Brandeis always remained alert to the inherent dangers of the simple expedient of governmental intervention. Bigness in government, for him, constituted the same threat as bigness in private power. "We risk our whole system," he believed, "by creating a power which we cannot control."

The Curse of Bigness—his consistent theme—has had an enduring importance throughout American history. The patriots of 1776 questioned whether they could preserve their unalienable rights in the large sphere of the British Empire. Can the United States in the twentieth century, with its highly industrialized, varied society, and its complex involvement in world affairs, conform to traditional democratic and libertarian values? If it is to do so, then Brandeis's concern for a regular accounting of public and private power, and his emphasis on decentralization, is crucial. Bigness was neither always better nor was it an absolute measure of progress for Brandeis. "Progress," he said, "must proceed from the aggregate performances of individual men"; in turn, he called for the application of "wisdom and ingenuity to adjust our institutions to the wee size of man and thus render possible his growth and development."

For Brandeis, this was the key toward preserving and enriching the American experiment in liberty; and thus he captured the essence of the spirit of 1776 in an idea that must remain eternally relevant for a free society.

John L. Lewis

MELVYN DUBOFSKY

For two decades John L. Lewis was the most powerful and feared labor leader in the United States. From Franklin D. Roosevelt's New Deal through Harry Truman's Fair Deal (1933–1952), Lewis defied Presidents, challenged congresses, intimidated employers, and threatened national crises. "His passing," wrote Lewis's biographer Saul Alinsky in 1949, "will mean the end of an era. It will be greeted with curses and feelings of deliverance from a life-long plague."

A story, certainly apocryphal, illustrates Lewis's fame. One morning as he left his suburban Alexandria home, Lewis paused, bent over, and tied a shoelace. Simultaneously a tourist bus stopped in front of the Lewis home; the passengers peered intently at the bent figure of the large man on the sidewalk. Lewis turned to a companion and remarked: "Even the behind of John L. Lewis is of national interest!"

Yet at the time of his death in June 1969, Lewis had become, for most Americans, a relic from the dim past. Perhaps it is now time to inquire anew about precisely what kind of man John L. Lewis was. Perhaps it is also time to ask again how well he served his followers, the nation, and American traditions.

Frankly, it is difficult to evaluate Lewis, partly because of myths of his own making and partly because of the oscillations in his career. Preferring to liken himself to Abraham Lincoln whose birthdate he shared (February 12), Lewis found himself most often compared to Hitler, Stalin, and Mussolini. Characterized by many before 1933 as a singularly conventional trade unionist, Lewis acted during the mid-1930s as the most militant, radical, and innovative of labor leaders. Praised by many as loyal to his friends, devoted to his family, and compassionate to his enemies, Lewis once personally declared to a union rival: "I never forget a friend, and I find it increasingly difficult to forget an enemy." Friendly to employers, welcomed by Washington society, often a pretentious social climber, Lewis fought vigorously to liberate workers from industrial slavery and to extend to them the full blessings of American liberty. How, then, does one penetrate the Lewisian enigma wrapped in a riddle cloaked in mystery?

The first child of Welsh immigrant parents (Thomas and Ann Louisa Watkins Lewis), John was born on Lincoln's birthday 1880 in the small Welsh immigrant coal-mining community of Lucas County, Iowa. His family moved persistently from one small central Iowa mine and farm town to another, though they settled for a while in Iowa's largest city, Des Moines, where Lewis attended city schools, completing all but the final year of high school. In 1897 the Lewis family returned to Lucas County, where the father rented a farm on which John and two of his brothers labored. A farm life, combined with part-time winter coal mining, was not unnatural considering that Lewis's Welsh paternal ancestors had been farmers.

As a young man, John also played baseball, debated, and managed the Lucas opera house, where he polished his talent for theatrics. In 1900, however, he decided to strike out on his own, leaving home to spend five years in the mountain West to toil in coal and metal mines, work on construction, and even try his hand at business. Much the wiser perhaps, if not the wealthier, Lewis returned to Lucas in 1905.

Back home, John joined the Masons, courted the local doctor's daughter, opened a grain and feed business, and ran for political office. He proved successful in fraternal and personal affairs—not in business or politics. The Masons elected him an officer and the doctor's daughter—Myrta Edith Bell—married him in June 1907; but the panic of 1907 wiped out his grain enterprise and the voters of Lucas rejected his bid for the mayor's office. Though a failure in business and politics, Lewis was still a young man (twenty-eight) when he chose a career in trade unionism.

In 1908 the entire Lewis family moved to Panama, Illinois, a newly opened mining village. There all the Lewis men found work in the mines and John used family connections to build a local union machine that brought him first the local union presidency, then a paid appointment with the state mine workers' organization, and finally a job with Samuel Gompers and the American Federation of Labor (AFL).

Always ready to seize the main chance, Lewis used his link with Gompers to rise in the United Mine Workers. In 1917 he became UMW statistician and editor of the union journal; a year later he obtained an acting vice presidency; and in 1919 he became acting president. Thus, within four years, Lewis had risen from obscurity to the leadership of the nation's largest trade union, the Mine Workers, which in 1919 claimed over 400,000 members. No one had ever practiced trade union politics with greater success.

The 1920s, a decade of unsurpassed prosperity, were filled with paradox and irony for Lewis. As the nation prospered, the coal industry and its workers suffered. The price of coal collapsed, production stagnated, and miners lost their jobs. Although Lewis consolidated his personal power within the UMW, becoming by 1930 the undisputed, autocratic ruler of the miners' union, the organization then numbered only 60,000 members, a loss of 500,000 during Lewis's ten-year reign as president.

Outside of the union, too, nothing Lewis did during the 1920s worked. Coal operators, much as Lewis wooed them, refused to bargain with a weak union. Presidents Coolidge and Hoover appreciated Lewis's endorsements, but they rebuffed a labor leader whose following and influence steadily slipped. Yet Lewis in 1932 endorsed Hoover for reelection, a peculiar choice in a depression year election Franklin D. Roosevelt and the Democrats were certain to win.

Then in perhaps the most paradoxical development in Lewis's career, during the Great Depression, the labor leader not only rebuilt the miners' union but also organized millions of workers in the auto, steel, rubber, and other mass-production industries. By cooperating with the Roosevelt administration, Lewis rejuvenated the UMW between June and September 1933. Always the gambler, Lewis planned to spend *all* the labor movement's resources in an attempt to organize millions of workers hitherto outside the labor movement. Realizing that the New Deal provided an unequaled opportunity to unionize the bulk of the nation's blue-collar workers, Lewis pleaded with other AFL labor leaders to join him in organizing the unorganized. When the AFL old-guardsmen proved too cautious to organize what some among them referred to as "the rubbish at labor's door," Lewis challenged them, created the Congress of Industrial Organizations (CIO), and unionized the mass-production workers.

Lewis's great gamble paid off. Founded in November 1935, the CIO by November 1937 claimed more members than the AFL. Moreover, in 1937 the CIO won union contracts in autos (General Motors) and steel (United States Steel) from the nation's two most intransigent openshop, antiunion corporations. In less than two years, Lewis's organization achieved what the AFL had failed to win in half a century.

As CIO conquered autos, steel, rubber, the waterfront trades, and other industries in 1937, one observer wrote: "Around mammoth modern mills and at bleak old factories, on ships and on piers, at offices and in public gathering-places, men and women roared, 'CIO! CIO!' . . . Labor was on the march as it had never been before in the history of the Republic."

They also chanted "Lewis! Lewis! Lewis!" as the CIO leader played the bellowing proletarian bull to Roosevelt's mellifluous, patrician aristocrat. Throughout the New Deal's halcyon years, Lewis and Roosevelt performed for the same audiences, smote the same targets (economic royalists), and struck the same tender chords among workingmen and women. In both cases, the men and the times resonated.

1937 was the acme of Lewis's career. He received as much acclaim as Roosevelt, some commentators pointing to him as labor's first likely presidential candidate. In January 1937, *Nation* magazine placed Lewis on its honor roll for 1936 "for continuing to give strength and backbone to the American labor movement." Heywood Broun, the popular columnist, compared him to Joe Louis, the Negro heavyweight champion, the "brown bomber" and idol of the black masses. Because of the CIO's success in organizing black workers, quipped Broun, "I think Lewis [John L.] is the greatest heavyweight of our day." "It seems to me," wrote another columnist, "that in the second half of this decade [1930s] the most significant leader in American society will be John Lewis."

Lewis's fame and power flowed from the fact that under his leadership, workers had become an effective mass force in economics and politics for the first time in American history. Never before had the basic industries had to share power and authority with representatives of their employees. The Roosevelt Democratic coalition, the beneficiary of over half a million dollars in UMW-CIO funds during the 1936 election, seemed dependent on Lewis's organized labor army. If Lewis succeeded in organizing the 20-30 million workers he asserted were ready to join CIO, the emergence of a labor party and the election of a labor president seemed plausible. Lewis had not only liberated workers from industrial serfdom; he had made them a political power, proving that industrial and political democracy were inseparable.

Yet by 1940 Lewis had split with Roosevelt, resigned his CIO presidency, and allied with conservative critics of the New Deal. Why? Perhaps because Lewis and Roosevelt, so much alike and yet so different, were the captives of forces beyond their control, victims in a minor Greek tragedy.

However much he believed himself a reformer and tribune for the people, President Roosevelt implemented policies designed to preserve the existing American social and economic order. However much he accommodated businessmen and extolled free enterprise and the profit system, Lewis represented workers who demanded a greater share of the nation's abundance and more control over their work and lives. Captives of their respective and divergent supporters, Roosevelt and Lewis were fated to clash in a conflict that boded ill for the New Deal, American workers, and the nation.

His feud with Roosevelt led Lewis to take the greatest gamble of his life in 1940. In a step that took most of the nation—especially workers—by surprise, Lewis asked citizens to vote for Wendell Willkie, "the barefoot boy from Wall Street." Indeed Lewis demanded that workers choose between himself and Roosevelt. If Roosevelt were reelected for a third term, Lewis pledged to resign as president of CIO. Assuming that he had enough influence among workers to swing a substantial bloc of votes to the Republicans in what figured to be a close election, Lewis miscalculated. The election was less than tight; Roosevelt ran most strongly in working-class precincts, including coal-mining regions. Rejected politically, Lewis kept his pledge and at the CIO convention November 1940, stepped down as president.

With his resignation from the CIO presidency and the departure of the UMW from CIO two years later, Lewis relinquished much of his stature and power as a labor leader. Thereafter, until he retired as UMW president in 1960, he engaged in incessant guerilla warfare against other labor leaders, Congress, and the White House. During World War II and immediate postwar years, Lewis, despite presidential, congressional, and popular opposition, practiced his belief that power was the only real morality. Although many Americans "damned his coal black soul" for calling out the coal miners on the eve of Pearl Harbor and again in 1943, Lewis remembered that during World War I miners had suffered by waiting to strike until after the war ended. Acting when power was his, Lewis through strikes in 1943, 1945, and 1946 won for UMW members wages, hours, and fringe benefits enjoyed by no other American workers.

Lewis's triumphs in the 1940s proved as ephemeral for coal miners as had been his consolidation of union power during the 1920s. The technological innovations that guaranteed high wages and juicy fringe benefits also reduced the need for coal miners. Once again during the 1950s, the membership, income, and influence of the UMW shrank. Indeed Lewis spent his final ten years as union leader watching the decline of the labor empire he had built. Fortunately Lewis died before his chosen successor William A. "Tony" Boyle and other UMW officials were found guilty of the murder of union insurgent Joseph Yablonski, his wife, and daughter, and before a union election supervised by the labor department resulted in the defeat of the machine John L. Lewis had built.

How, then, does one assess John L. Lewis's contribution to American workers, the nation, and its democratic heritage? Certainly during the 1920s he benefited no one but himself. During the 1930s, however, Lewis, more than any other individual, brought masses of industrial workers into the labor movement and altered fundamentally their relation to their jobs and employers. For millions of workers, long the subjects of industrial servitude, Lewis acted as the "Great Emancipator." In building CIO and compelling such industrial giants as General Motors and United States Steel to treat their workers as humans, not dispensable machines, Lewis perhaps did more than Franklin Roosevelt and the New Deal to transform the structure of American society by spreading industrial democracy. Whatever the twists and turns of Lewis's subsequent career, it must be stressed that few people, if any, accomplished so much in so short a time as he did in creating CIO and establishing mass-production unionism in the United States.

Many labor leaders and entrepreneurs, like Lewis, have been self-made men who have risen from obscurity to fame and wealth. Few, however, have been movers and shakers. No other individual in the history of the American labor movement equalled Lewis's mass appeal, brought industrial democracy to as many workers, or acted less obsequiously in the presence of presidents and industrialists. Whatever his shortcomings, and they were many, Lewis served the American nation and its people well during a particularly trying historical moment—the Great Depression—and he always acted as, in his own words, "something of a man."

Walter Lippmann

RONALD STEEL

Walter Lippmann was America's greatest journalist. He wrote better and wielded a greater influence than any other journalist in the history of the nation. Although he prided himself on being a newspaperman, he was also something else. As the author of more than twenty books, he probed beneath the questions of the day. In these books he was able to stand back from the headlines and put the events of a troubled era into perspective. There has never been anyone like him in the history of American letters, and it is unlikely that there ever will be again.

"I have lived two lives," Lippmann once said. "One of books and one of newspapers." Each helped the other. In the books that he wrote over a sixty-year career that began in 1910 he evolved the philosophy that he tested in his columns. In the syndicated column that he wrote for thirty-six years until his semi-retirement in 1967, he tried out the ideas that were then woven into his books. What was remarkable about Lippmann is that he lived these two lives at the same time. Each enriched the other and gave him an authority that no other newspaperman has ever approached.

His columns, which appeared several times weekly in the most important papers in America and throughout the world, were scrutinized in every embassy and foreign office. Even his critics found it impossible *not* to read Lippmann—if only to be able to refute him. Presidents came to him for advice, ambassadors presented their credentials at his Washington home, journalists and scholars beseeched him for interviews. During the six decades of his career he became an American institution.

Part of his success lay precisely in his ability to fuse his two worlds. He had a newspaperman's genius for clarification and a philosopher's gift for seeing the eternal reality behind the flickering headline. In a literary style that was a marvel of clarity and grace he gave meaning to the incessant bombardment of facts. He knew that there was a difference between news and truth, between information and education. "The press is no substitute for institutions," he once wrote. "It is like the beam of a searchlight that moves restlessly about, bringing one episode and then another out of the darkness into vision. Men cannot do the work of the world by this light alone."

Although he accepted the limitations of the press, he insisted that it was essential to the survival of democracy. "All that the sharpest critics of democracy have alleged is true if there is no steady supply of trustworthy and relevant news," he wrote in 1920. "Incompetence and aimlessness, corruption and disloyalty, panic and ultimate disaster, must come to any people which is denied an assured access to the facts. No one can manage anything on pap. Neither can a people."

Lippmann never gave his readers pap. He told them the harshest truths because he was convinced that a free people could not survive on illusions any more than they could on lies. "The war for liberty is an eternal struggle," he wrote fifty years ago.

One day liberty has to be defended against the power of wealth, on another day against the dead hand of bureaucrats, on another against the patrioteer and the militarist, on another against the profiteer, and then against the hysteria and passions of mobs, against obscurantism and stupidity, against the criminal and against the overrighteous. In this campaign every civilized man is enlisted till he dies, and he only has known the full joy of living who somewhere and at some time has struck a decisive blow for the freedom of the human spirit.

But . . . it is not enough to vindicate liberty in legislatures, in courts, in the press, in school boards, and before public opinion. There is a personal discipline necessary to the use of liberty. Without the discipline men never will love liberty and never will cherish it. They will be like a savage who by accident finds a delicate instrument and carelessly throws it away.

To be free the people had to know the facts. But beyond the facts there was the larger reality. It was this larger reality to which Lippmann addressed himself and which he elucidated to his readers.

In a sense his whole career was a search for order, a guiding principle that would impose a pattern on the incessant bombardment of facts. As a very young man he found that pattern in socialism, then in his idealistic involvement in the war that was supposed to "make the world safe for democracy," then in philosophical detachment from the follies of the Jazz Age. During the New Deal he shifted to the right and became an arch-opponent of what he called "collectivism." Yet during the fifties he attacked McCarthyism and the ideological crusading of the Cold War, and near the end of his career regained his youthful passion by becoming a vehement critic of the Vietnam war.

Although many tried to put a label on Lippmann, no one ever succeeded. He defied categorization either as a liberal or as a conservative. To his mind they were not opposites, but two aspects of a single philosophy. "Every truly civilized and enlightened American is conservative and liberal and progressive," he once wrote in a classic statement.

A civilized American is conservative in that his deepest loyalty is to the Western heritage of ideas which originated on the shores of the

Mediterranean Sea. Because of that loyalty he is the indefatigible defender of our own constitutional doctrine, which is that all power, that all government, that all officials, that all parties and all majorities are under the law—and that none of them is sovereign and omnipotent.

The civilized American is a liberal because the writing and the administration of the laws should be done with enlightenment and compassion, with tolerance and charity, and with affection.

And the civilized man is progressive because the times change and the social order evolves and new things are invented and changes occur. This conservative who is a liberal is a progressive because he must work and live, he must govern and debate in the world as it is in his own time and as it is going to become.

In his own life Lippmann had no trouble reconciling these three categories. They were the lodestars that allowed him to stand apart from political parties and popular passions. They allowed him to be a socialist at one time in his life, an economic conservative at another, a defender and then a critic of Franklin Roosevelt, a political realist who extolled military power yet urged a Cold War settlement with the Russians, an ardent exponent of the "national interest" who condemned ideological obsessions and "globalist" interventions.

Although he was a cosmopolitan and elegant man who moved easily in the world's capitals, he remained an ardent American patriot. His love for America did not take the form of jingoism. He deplored those who asserted their patriotism by questioning that of other Americans, or by denigrating other countries. Rather he extolled the dream of America where men stood equal before the law and equal before one another, an America that inspired the world by its example, not by the force of its arms. For this reason he was saddened and angered by the war in Vietnam which he saw as the betrayal of American ideals abroad. "We are not able to run the world and we shouldn't pretend that we can," he said in 1965. "We have neglected our own affairs. Our education is inadequate, our cities are badly built, our social arrangements are unsatisfactory. We can't wait another generation."

Lippmann wanted Americans to pursue the high ideals which had inspired the nation's founders and animated its greatest leaders. But he never ceased to remind them that the path was arduous and the goal elusive. He did not preach; it was not his temperament. He knew, as he once wrote, that if the moralist "is to deserve a hearing among his fellows, he must set himself this task which is so much humbler than to command and so much more difficult than to exort: he must seek to anticipate and to supplement the insight of his fellow men into the problems of their adjustment to reality."

What made Lippmann so provocative were the tensions in his own thought: the tensions between his books and his columns, between his quest for order and his enthusiasm for experimentation, between his suspicion of popular majorities and his abiding faith in democracy. While he believed in popular rule, he was never sentimental about it; he did not assume that the majority was always right. "Because a whole people clamors for war and gets it," he wrote in 1916, "there is no ground for calling the war democratic."

From his own experience in writing propaganda in the First World War he had seen at firsthand how people could be swayed by innuendo, distortion, and lies. He had seen how nations could be led to war and how mass emotions, once unleashed, could undermine the very democratic freedoms for which the war was ostensibly fought. When he returned from France in 1919 to find America in the grips of the Red Scare and Wilson's Fourteen Points—which he had helped write—ignored by the victors at Versailles, he was deeply disillusioned. Never again would he enlist in a crusade or trust the popular passions of the moment. He had seen how easily those passions could be manipulated.

His landmark study, *Public Opinion*, published in 1922, reflected this skepticism about the wisdom of transient majorities. It provided the ground work for the distinction he always made between the counting of heads and the counting of souls. "While nobody can seriously maintain that the greatest number must have the greatest wisdom or the greatest virtue," he wrote during the Scopes "monkey" trial in 1926, "there is no denying that under modern social conditions they are likely to have the most power."

For this reason he favored the kind of restrictions on majority rule written into the U.S. Constitution. "The genius of the American system," he wrote, "is that it limits all power—including the power of the majority." While he insisted that democracy was the best form of government, he believed that people had to be protected from their own emotions, and from manipulation by vested interests—even by their own government. "We must," he said in a tribute to George Washington, "refuse to identify the cause of freedom, justice and good government with the rule of the majority." Beyond the majority was an even greater principle that stood at the center of the American idea: "that the sovereignty of the people is never absolute, that the people are under the law, and that the people may make no law which does not conform to that higher law which has been gradually revealed to the awakening conscience of mankind." This is the theme of his last major book, *The Public Philosophy,* the classic statement of his faith in a higher law—beyond men, beyond majorities, beyond governments.

Lippmann was not always right in his enthusiasms or his assessments of people. But his record was remarkably high, and week after week, column after column, book after book, he set a standard to which many have aspired but none ever attained. He showed what journalism was capable of being, and he never tired of addressing the millions of unseen readers whom he believed cared as much as he about the great public issues with which free men had to concern themselves.

Both a liberal and a conservative, an expositor of Jeffersonian liberty and Hamiltonian authority, Lippmann urged Americans to resolve the tension between the two principles by uniting them. "Neither can live alone," he wrote.

> Alone, that is, without the other, each is excessive and intolerable. Freedom, the faith in man's perfectibility, has always and will always in itself lead through anarchy to despotism. Authority, the conviction that men have to be governed and not merely let loose, will in itself always lead through arbitrariness and corruption to rebellion and chaos. Only in their union are they fruitful. Only freedom which is under strong law, only strong law to which men consent because it preserves freedom, can endure.

With his commitment to reason, justice, and tolerance, Walter Lippmann was the most eloquent exponent of the spirit of 1776, and his long career was its living embodiment.

Martin Luther King, Jr.

HOWARD ZINN

Most Americans, listening in the summer of 1963 to the thundering baritone of Martin Luther King, Jr., on the steps of the Lincoln Memorial in Washington, unsettled by his repeated "I have a dream . . . ," were moved to think of the long quest of black people for equality. In the perspective of the Bicentennial of the American Revolution, what King spoke of that day may be seen as part of a larger dream of all Americans. That dream is of life, liberty, and the pursuit of happiness, promised in the early years of the Revolution but laid aside in the practical requirements of a Constitution catering to the propertied elements of that time.

Thus, Martin Luther King, characterized usually as the preeminent spokesman for black America of the 1950s and 1960s, may also be, in the annals of history, a spokesman for the unfulfilled expectations of all Americans, white and black, who have come through 200 years of national history and find themselves still in the midst of racial turmoil, economic distress, and international violence. If the problem of America is more than race, if inequality is a matter of class and sex and age as well as color, if there is a moral issue unresolved by the dry lines of the statute books and requiring the united action of masses of people, if social change requires the healing balm of good will as well as the power of confrontation and sacrifice—then King may be seen in history as one of the early voices of a new American revolution.

In 1954, the Supreme Court decision in *Brown* v. *Board of Education* had reinterpreted the Constitution's Fourteenth Amendment, to outlaw state statutes calling for segregated schools. But the law is not self-enforcing. A year later, in Montgomery, Alabama, Martin Luther King and thousands of black residents of that old slave city made the words of the Constitution crackle with the electricity of social struggle; they began to create the national climate which would make those words real.

The city of Montgomery had a law requiring segregation on buses. This was quite clearly in opposition to the Fourteenth Amendment, which prohibits states from discriminating on grounds of race. But laws, however unconstitutional, need to be challenged to be declared void. And if these laws are supported, as were the segregation laws of southern cities and states, by centuries of tradition and the sentiments of the white majority, that challenge would clearly need to have commanding power.

In Montgomery, such power developed out of the simple stubbornness of one woman, Rosa Parks, who, on December 1, 1955, refused to move from a seat reserved for whites on a city bus, saying later that she was "tired." Her arrest mobilized the city's Negro community for a boycott of the buses, led by a number of local leaders, including the new young pastor of the Dexter Avenue Baptist Church, Martin Luther King, Jr. King took that small word "tired" uttered by Rosa Parks, and brandished it before an audience of four thousand Montgomery Negroes gathered after the arrest:

128

But there comes a time when people get tired. We are here this evening to say to those who have mistreated us so long that we are tired—tired of being segregated and humiliated, tired of being kicked about by the brutal feet of oppression. We have no alternative but to protest. . . .

The Montgomery bus boycott worked. The Negro community, largely barred from voting, earning half the average income of whites, organized taxi and car pools, stayed off the buses for twelve months, and made their point. A Supreme Court decision settled the matter: the city segregation ordinance was declared unconstitutional. And Martin Luther King became known to the nation and the world as the symbol of nonviolent organized mass action to win equal rights.

What was the source of King's impetus to action? Although his father was a prominent Atlanta minister, he had known the humiliation of race arrogance—forced, as a high school debater, to surrender his seat to white passengers while returning from Valdosta, Georgia, to Atlanta, compelled once to sit behind a curtain in a railroad dining car, called "nigger" by a foreman during a summer job while in college.

What to do with his anger was suggested by diverse intellectual experiences after high school: reading Thoreau's *Civil Disobedience* at Morehouse College, learning about Gandhi's nonviolence while at Crozer Theological Seminary, studying Marx's analysis of the exploitation in industrial capitalism, wrestling with Reinhold Niebuhr's idea that pacifism was not enough, that defense against tyranny requires positive action. With a doctorate in philosophy from Boston University, King nevertheless did not surrender that skepticism of pure reason he had developed at Morehouse College, when he wrote in the student journal that "education which stops with efficiency may prove the greatest menace to society. The most dangerous criminal may be the man gifted with reason, but with no morals."

After the Montgomery events, King traveled to Europe to meet President Nkrumah, of Ghana, and to India to meet Nehru. He then returned to Atlanta to work on founding the Southern Christian Leadership Conference (SCLC), in which King and Ralph Abernathy, his fellow pastor in Montgomery, would join other ministers and laymen for the next decade in the struggle against racial segregation. SCLC helped the black college veterans of the 1960 sit-ins to found the Student Nonviolent Coordinating Committee.

SNCC became the militant wing of the civil rights movement in the sixties, working with King but also criticizing him for his occasional compromises with the cautious policies of the national administration. During the 1961 Freedom Rides, King supported Attorney General Robert Kennedy's idea of a cooling-off period. Later that year, he favored the more moderate tactic for SNCC of working on voter registration rather than direct confrontation of segregated facilities.

Montgomery had showed the advantages of mobilizing the black population of a whole city. In late 1961, King traveled to the old-South town of Albany, Georgia, to support a mass movement that had developed there. It had been initiated in part by a few SNCC activists, to end segregation in transportation and other facilities. Seven hundred Albany Negroes and a few whites had been jailed for marching and gathering, nonviolently, to protest racial discrimination. King joined them and was arrested too. But when the series of confrontations was over in late 1962, Albany Negroes had gained very little, and there grew a sober realization that King depended too much on dramatic tactics of attack and withdrawal. He did not seem to have a long-term strategy of digging into a community and working slowly, patiently to change thought and institutions, as SNCC organizers were beginning to do in various places in the Deep South.

The mass demonstrations King and his associates organized in the tightly segregated, highly industrialized city of Birmingham, Alabama, in the spring of 1963, were more successful than those in Albany. All over the world, people saw the photos of Birmingham police arresting Negroes for marching towards city hall, using high-pressure water hoses on demonstrators, turning police dogs on children. Six thousand black children, from six to sixteen, had marched through the streets and a thousand were arrested. King too was arrested; his "Letter From A Birmingham Jail" was a brilliant defense of direct action and civil disobedience.

The outcome of the Birmingham marches was the desegregation of schools, lunch counters, libraries, and golf courses. But the economic subservience and political impotence of blacks in the city remained. World opinion had been touched, and the U.S. government was pushed towards stronger civil rights legislation. But King and other civil rights leaders began to realize that racism was deeply embedded in an economic and social structure, and would require more radical change than the desegregation of lunch counters.

King learned that lesson slowly. He still had some faith in the liberal wing of the Democratic Party. And so he joined in the careful control of the great gathering of 200,000 blacks and whites in Washington on August 28, 1963. He went so far as to approve the censoring and moderating of the angry words of John Lewis, the SNCC speaker that day. King's own speech "I Have a Dream," is one of the great orations of American history. It was a hundred years since the Emancipation Proclamation, King said, but "we must face the tragic fact that the Negro is still not free." The Negro was still segregated. The Negro was still poor. "The whirlwinds of revolt will continue to shake the foundations of our nation until the bright day of justice emerges." Nevertheless, King had a dream that some day things would be different. Again and again, to tumultuous applause, he sounded out the details of that dream. And then he closed:

> When we let freedom ring, when we let it ring from every village and every hamlet, from every state and every city, we will be able to speed up that day when all God's children, black men and white men, Jews and Gentiles, Protestants and Catholics, will be able to join hands and sing in the words of that old Negro spiritual, "Free at last! Free at last! Thank God almighty, we are free at last!"

But it was a long way from rhetoric to reality. In Oslo, Norway, December, 1963, King spoke to a distinguished audience:

> I accept the Nobel Prize for Peace at a moment when twenty-two million Negroes of the United States of America are engaged in a creative battle to end the long night of racial injustice. . . . I am mindful that debilitating and grinding poverty afflicts my people and chains them to the lowest rung of the economic ladder.

In between his Washington speech and his Oslo speech, a church in Birmingham was bombed, and four black children were killed. In 1964, even after an intense summer of civil rights activism in Mississippi, including the murder of three young civil rights workers, the nation's liberal

131

administration would not fight for the inclusion of blacks in the Mississippi delegation to the Democratic National Convention—and King did not seem strong enough to press that fight.

He was still attached to the southern struggle, and in 1965 marched with others, first stopped brutally by Alabama state troopers, then protected by a contingent of federal troops, to establish the right to march peacefully from Selma to Montgomery. That summer, Congress passed the Voting Rights Act, the strongest move yet to allow blacks to register to vote in the South. But the outbreak of black rioting that same summer in the Watts district of Los Angeles, where blacks could vote but still lived in poverty, suggested to King and other blacks that a revolution might be required to make America fulfill those promises King had declaimed on the steps of the Lincoln Memorial.

King's vision seemed to grow in the wake of two enormous events. One was the widespread ghetto riots of 1967, emphasizing to him that, whatever rights were stated in the opinions of the Supreme Court or the words of Congressional statutes, what was basic was the Negro's economic destitution. The second event was the war in Vietnam, which disturbed King profoundly. The same liberal government, of Kennedy and Johnson, which offered words but little real change for blacks, was mercilessly bombing the peasant villages of Vietnam. King began to break with the liberal establishment and to think in more radical ways.

Against all attempts by moderate blacks and powerful whites to silence him, he spoke out forcefully against the war. In the spring of 1967, speaking in New York, he connected the ghetto uprisings with Vietnam. Black youths, rioting against the conditions of the ghetto, had asked King—did not the U.S. government use massive violence to gain its ends? "Their questions hit home, and I knew that I could never again raise my voice against the violence of the oppressed in the ghettos without having first spoken clearly to the great purveyor of violence in the world today—my own government."

In early 1968, King continued to protest the Vietnam war. He also organized marches in Chicago against the slum conditions of Negroes there. He went to Memphis in March, after two black garbage workers were crushed to death in a machinery failure, and there joined the striking garbage workers. As he stood on a motel balcony, an unseen assassin shot him down.

At the time of his death, King seemed to be moving away from his faith in the good will of liberal leaders in Washington. He was beginning to see the need for long-range organizing from below to bring fundamental changes in economic arrangements, as well as in the laws and thought of the country.

This vision was the logical extension of King's continued insistence that justice was more important than law. It was also the logical extension of the critical, even revolutionary attitudes towards established authority stated in Jefferson's Declaration of Independence and Paine's *Common Sense*. It is a vision worth recalling in these days of the Bicentennial.

Epilog

American Revolution as a Creative Era

HENRY STEELE COMMAGER

Two great historical movements intersected in eighteenth-century America: one, vertical—the realization of centuries of English political thought and experiments which were institutionalized in American constitutionalism; the second, horizontal—the realization in the New World of much of the philosophy and the program of the European Enlightenment. America was the heir and the beneficiary of both of these intellectual and cultural movements and to both of them made important contributions. As might be expected, these contributions were not so much philosophical as practical and institutional.

British constitutionalism and the European Enlightenment not only intersected in America: they were interwoven, as heredity and environment are interwoven. If Americans depended largely on their inheritance for ideas, the ideas, in turn, depended very much on the American environment for their realization. England, and the ancient world, had formulated most of the principles and experimented with some of the practices of representative government, separation of powers, limits on governmental authority, federalism, and so forth, but it was only in the New World that these achieved their growth and maturity. Britain, France, the Germanies, and Italy imagined and agitated the ideas of religious toleration, humanitarianism, the supremacy of reason, progress, happiness, and enlightenment. But it was in the New World that these ideas found welcome and protection, and survived the great reaction we associate with the counterrevolution, Napoleon and the Holy Alliance.

Let us begin with the institutionalization of the political inheritance.

I

Thanks to their inheritance from the most enlightened of Old World nations—thanks to a century and a half of experience in self-government, in legislatures, town meetings, and county courts, Americans were by 1776 more mature politically than any other people on the globe, and more creative, too.

It is that creativity which impresses us most, perhaps because we are so uncreative today. It was, to be sure, chiefly institutional. Americans did not originate the ideas that Thomas Jefferson set forth with such matchless eloquence in the Declaration of Independence. Nor did they originate the *ideas* inherent in the new written constitutions and the bills of rights, or in the administrative mechanisms which they devised. These were part of the moral inheritance of Western man; they were—in the happy phrase of Thomas Paine—the *Common Sense* of the matter. Philosophically many of their ideas were commonplace. What was not commonplace, but unique, was that alone of the peoples who embraced the ideas of the Enlightenment, the Americans "realized the ideas of the wisest writers," (it is John Adams's phrase) and transformed ideas into institutions.

Those institutions embraced almost the whole world of government and politics. It is sobering to reflect that every major American political institution was invented before the year 1800 and that not one has been invented since that year.

Let us contemplate some of these innovations.

First, the Founding Fathers created a *nation*—something no people had ever done before, for heretofore nations had simply grown. "Thirteen clocks," said John Adams, "were made to strike together, a perfection of mechanism which no artist had ever before effected." In the face of all experience the new and artificially created nation survived. It survived, too, without those familiar stigmata of Old World nationalism—a monarch, a ruling class, a capitol, an established church, an army and a navy, and without that body of history and tradition and legends deemed to be essential to national unity. These latter Americans did manage to create with almost miraculous speed: heroes, villains, legends, myths, symbols, mottoes, even history—in short, a usable past.

But their real genius was for the practical, and their most significant achievements were in the realm of politics. Thus they solved, almost overnight, the two intractable problems of colonialism and of federalism. No Old World nation had known what to do with colonies except to exploit them for its own benefit. The new United States was born a great colonial power, with a hinterland larger than the original thirteen states; it was to be, in the course of the nineteenth century, the greatest of colonizing powers. What was to be its policy towards the hinterland which stretched westward to the Mississippi and then, in another generation, to the Pacific? Was the great West to be exploited for the benefit of the "mother country"? Happily wiser policies prevailed. By the simple device of transforming "colonies" into States and admitting them to the union on the basis of absolute equality with the original States, Americans substituted the principle of the coordinate state for the principle of colonialism.

They solved, too, the problem of federalism, that problem which had eluded every state from the days of the ancient Greek confederations down to the old British Empire. All previous federalisms had been either too strong at the center or in the parts. The Americans were wise enough to bypass the awkward question whether ultimate power inhered in the states or in the nation. Instead, by what we can now see was political originality of the highest order, they located sovereignty in the people themselves, people who, in turn, delegated some sovereign powers to their state governments and others to their new national government. This is a commonplace of politics now, but in all the literature of federalism from the Achaean League on to the insights of an Edmund Burke no one had ever come up with this idea before.

The Fathers realized that this distribution of powers between governments was fraught with danger, and they sought to circumvent that danger by another stunning invention. They provided that the Constitution should be "the supreme law of the land" and that "*judges* should be bound thereby." Thus, again for the first time in history, they placed upon

137

the judiciary authority to harmonize the conflicting claims of the different parts of the federal system.

All governments, the Declaration asserted, *derive* their just powers from the consent of the governed. It was an old idea, but had never yet been put into effect. And the great Blackstone, whose *Commentaries* (so Burke himself asserted) had sold as widely in America as in Britain, had made clear that "however just this . . . may be in theory, we cannot practically adopt it, nor take any *legal* steps for carrying it into execution under any dispensation of government now existing."

How, in fact, were the "governed" to give their consent, to make clear that they were indeed the source of all authority and entitled to make and unmake governments? And how were they to go about this without destroying all law? From the beginning Americans solved these problems as if by instinct. The principle that men make government was put into practice first in the Mayflower Compact, again in the Fundamental Orders of Connecticut of 1639, and thereafter on a score of frontiers all through the seventeenth, eighteenth, and even nineteenth centuries. Two examples must suffice. Here is a group of "mechanicks" of New York City in 1776, informing their representatives that

> To judge whether it be consistent with their interest to accept or reject a constitution framed for that state of which they are members . . . is the birthright of every man to whatever state he may belong. There he is, or ought to be, by inalienable right, a co-legislator with all the other members of that community.

Or listen to Richard Henderson addressing the representatives of four little frontier settlements out in Kentucky in 1775 whom he had called together to draw up a constitution:

> If any doubt remain amongst you with respect to the force or efficacy of whatever laws you now or hereafter make, be pleased to consider that all power is originally in the people . . . you are fixing the palladium, or placing the first cornerstone of an edifice [which] can only become great and glorious in proportion to the excellence of its foundation.

138

All of this philosophy and practice was shortly institutionalized into the constitutional convention, a contrivance which has some claim to be considered the most important political instrument of democracy, for it provides the essential mechanism whereby men can come together and create governments. More, it provides a logical method to "alter or abolish" governments—by adding amendments to a constitution, or by substituting a new constitution.

Thus, for the first time in history, men legalized revolution. As Alexander Hamilton wrote, the constitutional convention "substituted the mild magistracy of the law for the violent and sanguinary agency of the sword."

But history taught that all governments tended to aggrandize power. How place limits on government? No government in the Old World was, in fact, limited—certainly not that of Frederick the Great or of Catherine of Russia or of the successive Louises of France; not even that of George III and his Parliament.

This principle that government was in fact limited by the great laws of Nature and Nature's God, the Founding Fathers translated into a series of institutions. First they drew up written constitutions which bound government to those powers specifically granted. Second they provided for a real separation of powers and for a distribution of powers among the branches of government, which guaranteed both checks and balances. Within a few years they added something new in politics: judicial review of the constitutionality of both legislative and executive acts—a practice whose most spectacular recent example was U.S. vs. Nixon. And to make certain that no government would violate the rights of the people, they added to their constitutions, state and federal alike, bills of rights setting forth in detail just what rights were beyond the reach of government.

For all their practicality the new political and constitutional institutions were not self-functioning. It remained to create what is, in some ways, the central institution of democracy: the political party. Ever since the days of the ancient Greek city-states, there had been political organizations and divisions. But all of these were precisely those "factions" against which Washington—and so many others—incessantly warned.

The modern political party—the party as we know it in America, western Europe, and Japan—is an American invention which can be dated from the decade of the 1790s. What is perhaps most astonishing is that the party, as it emerged out of the American scene in that decade, took on, almost by instinct, those qualities which it has ever since retained, and which distinguished it most sharply from the cliques and factions of the Old World. First, the party took on responsibility for making the political mechanisms of government work in day-by-day affairs: the selection of candidates, the discussion of issues, the conduct of campaigns, getting out the vote, harmonizing legislative and executive policies, and reconciling state and national interests. Second, parties emerged at the outset as national—not local or sectional—as they still are. Third, just as the American parties did not merely reflect local or sectional interests, so they did not reflect ideological, religious, ethnic, class, or other differences. Almost from the beginnings the parties constituted common denominators of the American people. Fourth, because they were common denominators, two parties were sufficient—the ins and the outs, if you will; to this day America has a two-party, not a multiparty, system. And finally, in America—in contrast to nineteenth-century Britain—the parties grew from the bottom up, not from the top down. What this meant was that the parties were democratic in an active, not just a passive, fashion; they provided an opportunity for every man to play some part in the drama of democracy and the business of government.

This by no means exhausts the record of political creativity in the new republic, but it must suffice. No other nation—not even Britain—can display so remarkable an achievement.

II

Intellectually eighteenth-century America was very much part of the European Enlightenment. In the New World, as in the Old, philosophies embraced a common body of ideas, subscribed to a common body of laws, shared a common faith. First they embraced the Newtonian world, governed by laws of Nature and by Reason. An inevitable corollary to this was commitment to freedom of the mind—freedom from religious superstitions, the tyranny of the church, of the state, and of the academy.

They shared a third commitment: a humanitarianism which imagined and fought for the abolition of torture and the amelioration of the

140

barbarous penal code; an end to the Inquisition; the abolition of the slave trade and of slavery itself; improvement in medical and hospital care, in the lot of the peasants and the serfs everywhere; the beginnings of the emancipation of women and a new solicitude for childhood.

Their ultimate objective was the same everywhere: to liberate the minds of men and to conform so perfectly to the laws of Nature that the evils and corruptions which had for so long afflicted mankind would vanish, and man would enter a new golden age.

This was an exhilarating philosophy, but the agenda of the Old World philosophes was far from exhilarating. It was, as it turned out, almost wholly negative. For the Old World philosophes were helpless against the weaponry of the state and the law, the church and the Inquisition, the military and the universities, which bristled on every quarter of the horizon. These institutions could not be overthrown; they must somehow be circumvented. In most countries, therefore, the energies of the reformers were devoted to the elementary task of survival.

All the philosophers, European and American alike, were trained on the classics, and all knew Plato's prediction that there would be "no end to the troubles of states, or of humanity itself, until philosophers became kings in this world, or until those we call kings and rulers, really and truly became philosophers." There were no philosophers who were kings, though here and there there were kings who played at being philosophers—like Frederick of Prussia, or Catherine the Great, or Gustavus III of Sweden. The Americans had no kings—not after they had toppled George III anyway—but they had philosophers in plenty. And if the philosophers were not kings, they were something better: the elected representatives of a sovereign people. That was something new under the sun. In America, and perhaps alone in America, the people had deliberately chosen to be ruled by philosophers: Washington, John Adams, Jefferson, Madison in the presidential chair; a Bowdoin, a Jay, a Franklin, a Pinckney in the governors' offices. They were rulers—within the terms of the law—and they were philosophers. They did not need to curry favor with capricious monarchs; they could appeal, with some confidence, to an educated electorate; they were not required to spend their energies sweeping away the anachronisms which littered the landscape of history. In America they were able to translate their ideas into institutions—and did. This is the major difference between the Enlightenment in the New World and in the Old.

No need here to war against feudalism, because there was none. No need to topple a ruling class, because by Old World standards there was no ruling class—unless you place the whole of the white population in that category. Neither wealth, nor education, nor family could confer any *legal* privilege, only color. Under the Constitution of 1787 any free white man who was native-born and thirty-five could become president of the United States; anyone who was white could be a justice of the Supreme Court, secretary of state, or ambassador, no matter how rich or poor, how devout or agnostic, how learned or ignorant. No need to struggle against the power of the military: there was, in effect, no military; no need to combat censorship, for there was no censorship, or none that mattered. No need to agitate for the end of torture, for torture was unknown to American law. No need to campaign for the secularization of education: by Old World standards all education was secular; certainly none were excluded from college or university on religious grounds.

No need, even—once the Revolution was under way—to launch a crusade against the church. Nowhere in the Western world of the eighteenth century was there true freedom of religion. Americans were the first to establish not only true religious toleration but complete religious equality and complete separation of church and state.

Jefferson himself described the campaign for the separation of church and state in Virginia as "the severest contest in which I have ever been engaged." If that were true it would cast a roseate glow upon the American scene. For no one in Virginia lost his life in this struggle, none went to the stake or the galleys for his faith: there were no pogroms, no crusades. We cannot but wonder what the scores of philosophes who wore out their hearts in a vain struggle to overthrow the infamy would have thought of Jefferson's observation.

The Virginia Bill of Rights guaranteed the right not only to pursue but to obtain happiness, and Jefferson wrote happiness into the great Declaration. I like better his letter to the charming Maria Cosway congratulating her on the birth of a daughter:

> They tell me que vouz allez faire un enfant . . . you may make children there, but this is the country to transplant them to. There is no comparison between the sum of happiness there and here.

142

Jefferson knew what he was talking about. He had seen the pursuit of happiness in the Old World and he thought it, for the most part, a vain thing.

In the Old World, progress—like happiness—meant improvements in the arts and sciences and the gradual refinement of manners and morals. Certainly it was not anything that concerned the lower orders of society. Immanuel Kant made this clear. Progress, he said

> If it is to come, must come from above, not by the movement of things from the bottom to the top, but by the movement from the top to the bottom. . . . To expect to train men who can improve themselves by means of education of the youth in intellectual and moral culture is hardly to be hoped for.

But it was certainly something to be hoped for in America, which already boasted (in all likelihood) the most literate society on the globe, and all of whose leaders were educators. Consider Benjamin Franklin—the most persistent and effective champion of progress of his generation. To him progress was always practical. It meant better lighting, paved streets, more efficient stoves and lightning rods. It meant peace with the Indians, frontier defense, intercolonial union. It meant the Junto Library, the College of Philadelphia, Poor Richard's Almanac, and the American Philosophical Society. It meant the Albany Plan of Union, the Articles of Confederation, a Treaty of Alliance with France, the Federal Constitution. It meant moral progress, but that, too, was a practical matter: remember his box score of moral virtues! Franklin did not aim at Utopia but he tried to make Pennsylvania less class-ridden, less corrupt, less barbarous in its treatment of the Indian, more nearly a pleasant, agreeable, and prosperous society than any other, and he succeeded.

We do not commonly think of President Monroe as a spokesman for the American enlightenment. Yet he was very much a part of the revolutionary generation; a product of Virginia, the William and Mary College, the revolutionary struggle of Jefferson and Madison, and he lived all his life in the shadow of Monticello. Listen to him as he gives his first Inaugural Address, one which sums up much of the thinking of the American enlightenment:

143

Never did a government commence under auspices so favorable, nor ever was success so complete. If we look to the history of other nations, ancient or modern, we find no example of a growth so rapid, so gigantic; of a people so prosperous, and happy. In contemplating what we have still to perform, the heart of every citizen must expand with joy when he reflects how near our government has approached to perfection: that in respect to it we have no essential improvement to make, that the great object is to preserve it in the essential principles and features which characterize it, and that that is to be done by preserving the virtue and enlightening the minds of the people.

Perhaps if we could recover our virtue and enlighten the minds of the people, this might read, once again, as a prophecy rather than an elegy.

III

All of this may be regarded as a product of what we have come to call the spirit of '76. That spirit was not only bold, resolute, and courageous, it was creative, constructive, visionary, and imaginative. Through the nineteenth and well into the twentieth century it worked like a ferment, not only in the United States but throughout the globe: how impressive that it should be invoked not only by the French as they prepared for the great revolution of 1789 and by the many peoples of Latin America as they threw off the yoke of Spanish government in the early years of the nineteenth century, but in our own day by even the new nations of Rhodesia and North Vietnam. Clearly the eloquence of the Declaration still has the power to inspire and the principles of the Declaration the power to animate men throughout the globe.

Do they still have the power to inspire and to animate Americans as they prepare to move into the third century of their history as a nation?

The institutions which the Founding Fathers bequeathed to us have survived pretty well. We still live under the Constitution of 1787, and we still use the constitutional convention and the amending processes to change our constitutions, rather than resorting to force. We are still a federal union, though the nature of federalism has changed profoundly and

144

the center of political gravity is now in the nation, not the states. Government is still limited—in theory anyway—the judiciary is still independent, and judicial review plays a more important role in our history than at any time in the past. The guarantees of the Bill of Rights are respected in principle if not always in practice. Church and State are still separated and religious toleration is the common sense of the matter.

The most profound changes have come in the realm of the intangible—in the realm of attitudes, expectations, and beliefs. They take the form of widespread indifference to the "arrogance of power," to what Walt Whitman called "the never-ending audacity of elected persons," and to the very principle that government is limited and must observe its limits: a readiness to alienate what Jefferson assumed were "unalienable" rights; an attitude of acquiescence in repeated violations of the Bill of Rights—threats to freedom of speech and of the press, freedom of assembly and of petition, to those rights of privacy which were presumably set beyond the reach of government, and to the guarantees of due process of law and of equal protection of the laws. They can be read in the denial of real, as opposed to legal, equality to large segments of our society—equality in jobs, housing, education, and the benefits of medical care. They are obvious to outsiders in the assumption of superiority over other peoples and nations, in the shift of the sense of mission from moral examples and persuasion to economic pressure and military might, and in a readiness to concede the utmost claims of the military. They are painfully ostentatious in the growth of that corruption in government which the Fathers most feared—the vulgar corruption of exploiting office for private gain, the dangerous corruption of aggrandizing power for personal or party advantage. They confess themselves in a growing indifference to and ignorance of the heritage of the past—the past of that Greek and Roman history which entered into the very fabric of Revolutionary thought; the past of the American experience—the experience of those who built a civilization in a howling wilderness, those who won independence and created a nation, those who developed and protected and maintained that nation through the perilous years of its first century. No less ominous is the loss of faith in the future, the passing of that sense of fiduciary obligation to posterity which animated the generation of the Founding Fathers.

One tradition which we have lost or forfeited is the tradition of revolution itself. Except in the scientific and technological arena we are far less sympathetic to revolution—or even to change—than we were two centuries ago. Where we were once the beacon light of revolution to the oppressed peoples of the world, we are now the champions of stability, security, and the status quo; our attitude toward revolutions in Cuba, Santo Domingo, Guatemala, Greece, China, Vietnam is very much like that of the Holy Alliance toward the revolutions in Latin America at the beginning of the last century. Nor are we more sympathetic to revolution at home. What happened, we may ask, to that proud statement of Thomas Jefferson in his first Inaugural Address, "If there be any among us who would wish to dissolve this union, or to change its republican form, let them stand undisturbed as monuments of the safety with which error of opinion can be tolerated where reason is left free to combat it."

Perhaps the most conspicuous change that has affected our capacity to carry out the principles of the past and invent new principles for the future is in the realm of political leadership. When the new United States had a population of some three million—approximately half that of Chicago today—with no great urban centers, no great universities, no great newspapers, no professional class, it produced Franklin, Washington, John Adams, Jefferson, Madison, Hamilton, John Jay, John Marshall and—we may add those two refugees—Tom Paine and Albert Gallatin. Now, with a population of over two hundred millions, with all the great learned scientific institutions and vast cities, libraries, universities of an advanced civilization, we boast of no one who can be admitted to the company of the Founding Fathers.

When we ask whether we can revive the spirit of 1776, we are really asking whether we can find leaders who will provide us with principles and philosophies adequate to the needs of the next century, and whether the American people are sufficiently enlightened to embrace such principles and philosophies. Can we reanimate our sense of the past and our sense of dependence on it; can we rekindle that sense of fiduciary obligation to the generations ahead so essential if we are to avoid catastrophe? Can we solve those great domestic problems which glare ceaselessly upon us—problems of the waste of our resources; of the decay of our cities; of the growing disparity between the rich and the poor; or adequate care for the health, welfare, and education of all elements of society; or the restoration of the cities; of equal justice to all elements in society? These problems are difficult to solve, but no more difficult than were the problems which faced the generation of

146

Washington and Jefferson and which they managed to solve. Can we work out agreement with other peoples and nations of the globe so that we may solve the problems of interdependence? Can we cooperate with the other nations as the Founding Fathers cooperated with other states of the American union—to deal with the world crises of population, energy, pollution, atomic power and atomic war, of equalization of access to the necessities of life, of the protection of liberty and of individualism in a world that threatens to be too dangerous to allow liberty and too large and complex to tolerate individualism?

Perhaps we can do no better than repeat the touching appeal in Woodrow Wilson's first Inaugural Address:

> Men's hearts wait upon us; men's lives hang in the balance; men's hopes call upon us to say what we will do. Who shall live up to the great trust? Who dares fail to try?

Contributors

A. Owen Aldridge is professor of comparative literature at the University of Illinois. He has published several biographical studies, including *Man of Reason: The Life of Thomas Paine.*

Henry Steele Commager teaches at Amherst College. A well-known American historian, his numerous books have helped to educate a generation of students in the history of the United States.

Allen F. Davis is a member of the Department of History at Temple University. He has a special interest in the history of reform and is the author of a major study of Jane Addams, *American Heroine: The Life and Legend of Jane Addams.*

Vincent P. DeSantis is professor of American history at the University of Notre Dame. Recipient of both a Guggenheim fellowship and a Fulbright award, he has written extensively in the area of American political history; his most recent book is *The Shaping of Modern America, 1877–1916.*

Jay P. Dolan teaches U.S. urban and religious history at the University of Notre Dame. His first book, *The Immigrant Church: New York's Irish and German Catholics, 1815–1865,* was published in 1975.

Melvyn Dubofsky teaches American history at the State University of New York at Binghamton. He is the author of several works about American labor history, most notably *We Shall Be All: A History of the IWW.* He is currently completing a biography of John L. Lewis.

Wilbert R. Hasbrouck is a professional architect and a specialist in the restoration and preservation of historic buildings. He is the editor and publisher of *The Prairie School Review,* a journal of architectural history.

Matthew Josephson is the author of over twenty books, including *Edison: A Biography.* Living in retirement in Sherman, Connecticut, he continues his career as an historian and writer.

Stanley I. Kutler is professor of history at the University of Wisconsin-Madison. An authority in American legal history, he is the author of *The Supreme Court and The Constitution.*

Vincent P. Lannie is a professor of the history of education at the University of Notre Dame and author of several studies in American educational history including *Henry Barnard: American Educator*.

Patricia McNeal teaches American history at Indiana University at South Bend, Indiana. Her scholarly interests center on women, social change, and the history of the American peace movement.

Martin E. Marty, a recognized authority in American religious history, teaches at The University of Chicago. He is the author of numerous books, the most recent of which is *The Pro and Con Book of American Religion: A Bicentennial Argument*.

Merrill D. Peterson is professor of history at the University of Virginia and author of *Thomas Jefferson and the New Nation: A Biography*.

Benjamin Quarles is a professor of history at Morgan State University, Baltimore, Maryland. He has written or edited numerous books in black history including *Black Abolitionists*.

Thomas J. Schlereth teaches in the American Studies Program at the University of Notre Dame. He has a scholarly interest in cultural history that ranges from colonial architecture to metropolitan Chicago. His most recent publication is *The University of Notre Dame: A Portrait of Its History and Campus*.

Marshall Smelser is the author of several studies of the American Revolution, including *The Winning of Independence*. An avid baseball fan, he has recently published an authoritative biography of Babe Ruth, *The Life That Ruth Built*.

Ronald Steel is the author of *Pax Americana* and other books and articles in foreign policy. He is currently completing a biography of Walter Lippman.

Howard Zinn is a member of the Political Science Department at Boston University. He is the author of several studies pertaining to the civil rights movement including *S.N.C.C.: The New Abolitionists*.